976 Dro
ngoole, Glenn
essential Texas books : a
esentative selection of classic

28081582950
   $19.99   ocn880521013
              12/31/14

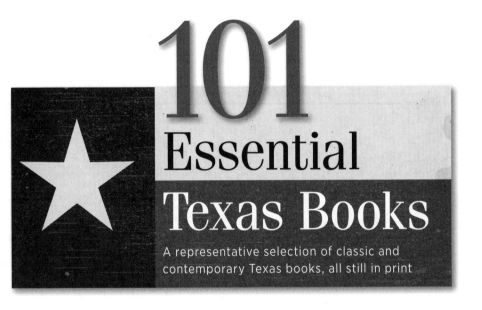

# 101
## Essential
## Texas Books

A representative selection of classic and
contemporary Texas books, all still in print

# Glenn Dromgoole
# & Carlton Stowers

Foreword by James Ward Lee

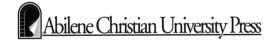

Abilene Christian University Press

## 101 Essential Texas Books

*A representative selection of classic and contemporary*
*Texas books, all still in print*

**ACU PRESS**

Copyright 2014 by Glenn Dromgoole & Carlton Stowers

ISBN 978-0-89112-324-8
LCCN 2014010907

Printed in the United States of America

LIBRARY OF CONGRESS CATALOGING-IN-PUBLICATION DATA
Dromgoole, Glenn.
   101 essential Texas books : a representative selection of classic and contemporary Texas books, all still in print / Glenn Dromgoole and Carlton Stowers ; foreword by James Ward Lee.
      pages cm
   Includes index.
   ISBN 978-0-89112-324-8
   1. Texas--Bibliography. 2. Best books--Texas. I. Stowers, Carlton. II. Title. III. Title: One hundred one essential Texas books. IV. Title: One hundred and one essential Texas books.
   Z1339.D76 2014
   [F386]
   016.9764--dc23
                                                                                        2014010907

Cover design and Interior text design by Sandy Armstrong, Strong Design

For information contact:
Abilene Christian University Press
1626 Campus Court
Abilene, Texas 79601

1-877-816-4455 toll free
www.acupressbooks.com

14  15  16  17  18  19  /  7  6  5  4  3  2  1

*To Carol Dromgoole & Pat Stowers*

# Contents

# Foreword

Just before he published *The 50 Best Books on Texas,* my late friend A. C. Greene told me, "Everyone loves a hit parade." He was right: the whole world loves a list— even trivial and frivolous lists like those found in supermarket tabloids: "The Ten Sexiest Men in the World," or "Ten Diets that Work," or "The One Hundred Most Intriguing People in America" (a list that always seems to include Henry Kissinger and Meryl Streep). Millions read these "hit parades," dumb though some of them are.

And then there are those wonderful and important lists that inform and enlighten, lists that tell of books we might have missed or historic events that help us see the world. The present compilation by Messers Dromgoole and Stowers is definitely one of the important lists. It is, of course, more than a mere list. Each of the 101 books featured is annotated with a full page of useful information. *101 Essential Texas Books* is the newest and best in a long line of bibliographies that Texas readers have seen come and go over the years. Think back to Sister M. Agatha's *Texas Prose Writings* (1936), Ramon Adams's various bibliographies of western cowboys and gunmen (several throughout the 1960s), and Florence Elberta Barns's *Texas Writers of Today* (1936). And then there is John Jenkins's famous *Basic Texas Books: An Annotated Bibliography of Selected Works for a Research Library.* In that volume of some 700 pages Jenkins lists books mostly out of print and mostly of interest to scholars of Texas history. But in various appendices, he does annotate a number of modern works. But great as that book is, it is not something that is accessible to what Virginia Wolfe calls "the common reader."

J. Frank Dobie produced *A Guide to Life and Literature of the Southwest* (1942, revised 1952), a very useful guide in its day to Texas and southwestern books, though many were out of print even back then. Another massive listing is *Southwestern Literature: A Bibliography* (1980), edited by John Q. Anderson et al. That volume attempts, partially successfully, to cover the subjects, the themes, and the individual writers of the Great Southwest.

And then we come to A. C. Greene's *The 50 Best Books on Texas* (1981), an eccentric but useful collection. Greene, always garrulous, often strays from the book he is annotating to tell what he was doing or thinking when the book came out. But it still makes for interesting and contentious writing.

*101 Essential Texas Books* avoids most of the pitfalls of its predecessors. The books are in print, the page-length annotations are crisp and clear, and the choices are ones that further our knowledge of Texas writing. Of course, every reviewer of the book will find something to quarrel with—why not a full treatment of J. Evetts Haley's *Charles Goodnight: Cowman and Plainsman?* What about Benjamin Capps's *A Woman of the People* (my all-time favorite Capps novel) instead of *The Trail to Ogallala?* Why limit the list to one book by a given writer?

But a patient reader will find in the "further readings" plenty of books about the Lone Star State. There's food, entertainment, folklore, history, and literature. One last thing: the compilers are too modest. No list of Texas books should fail to include Dromgoole's *A Small Town in Texas* or his recent *Coleman Springs USA.* And certainly any list of Texas books must annotate at least three by Carlton Stowers—his two award-winning true crime books and his wonderful *Where Dreams Die Hard,* the story of six-man football in Penelope, "the little town east of West." Okay. That is my gripe about this fine book. I have no others. So there!

*James Ward Lee*
*Fort Worth*

# Introduction

First of all, let's make it clear what this list of *101 Essential Texas Books* isn't. It isn't necessarily the Best Texas Books. It isn't the Greatest Texas Books of All Time. It isn't the collective choice of a panel of academic experts as to what constitutes Great Texas Literature.

We'll leave Best or Greatest to someone else. What we have set out to do here is offer a list of 101 Texas books, still in print, that we believe provide a balanced representation of Texas history, culture, and literature. Our recommendations cover a wide range of genres and classifications—fiction and non-fiction, classic and contemporary, cookbooks and children's books, books on sports, crime, personalities, and nature.

Our objective is not so much to rank the books as to call readers' attention to the wealth of good books about Texas, most written by Texas writers, many of whom are still living and writing and producing more good work. If you are interested in building a modern library of Texas books, or just reading some books you might not know about, this list suggests a place to begin.

In addition to the 101 books that head the listing, we have mentioned and indexed another 250 or so worthy of attention, and no doubt could have included many more. Some of those books are noted at the end of a review on a similar book, while others are grouped as "Some Other Notable Titles" at the end of each section.

Several other points we should make up front:

First, we have tried to make sure that every title on our list of *101 Essential Texas Books* is still actively in print. We did not include books that can only be found through rare book dealers or used book sales. Of course, these days with print-on-demand and e-book technology, books can be kept in circulation virtually forever, so a lot of classic Texas titles are still readily available today.

Second, in order to include as many authors as possible, we imposed a rule that we would limit an author to one entry in a category. For example, we selected just one novel each by Elmer Kelton, Larry McMurtry, Cormac McCarthy, and others, even though they have several worthy of inclusion. Instead, we incorporated some of their other titles into the pieces we wrote about them. The only exceptions to that rule were that in a few cases we included two entries by an author, but in different categories.

Third, we selected quite a few anthologies for our list because they offer a diversity and breadth in subject matter, authors, ethnicity, geography, and style. We have a dozen anthology collections, such as *Lone Star Literature*, with more than sixty essays and stories by twentieth century Texas writers. It ought to be in any self-respecting Texas library. *Texas in Poetry 2* has works by more than 150 Texas poets. *Lone Star Sleuths* offers excerpts from about thirty murder mysteries from Texas pens. *Twentieth-Century Texas* is a collection of essays by fifteen historians on topics that haven't received much attention in traditional history books.

Fourth, if we included a two-volume history or a series of books on a theme, we counted that as one entry. Mike Cox's comprehensive two-volume history of the Texas Rangers counted as one entry. The *Texans All* series on the five principal cultural groups in Texas—one entry. The series on *Literary Fort Worth, Literary Austin, Literary El Paso*, etc.—one entry. The wonderful *Hank the Cowdog* books by John Erickson—one entry.

Fifth, about sixty percent of the titles on our list have been published in the past ten to fifteen years. In recent years Texas has enjoyed an explosion of books on Texas themes from Texas writers, with university presses leading the charge and national publishers picking up on the growing market for regional titles. Events like the Texas Book Festival, West Texas Book Festival, and other local and regional fairs and booksellers—as well as Texas' prominent presence on the national stage—have helped ensure that Texas books get the recognition they deserve.

Putting together a list of recommended Texas books isn't a new idea by any means. Other observers and critics of Texas literature have undertaken similar listings over the years. Thirty years ago A. C. Greene picked his *50 Best Books on Texas*, which he revised a few years later to be the *50+ Best Books on Texas*. John H. Jenkins chronicled *Basic Texas Books* in 1983 and 1988 (no fiction) and Mike Cox added *More Basic Texas Books* a decade or so later. James Ward Lee in 1987 published a great summary on *Classics of Texas Fiction*. Some of the books they cite are no longer in print, but we have benefited from those selections and commend them to you.

We should also mention that we have excluded reference books and textbooks from our list. *The Handbook of Texas* published by the Texas State Historical Association is a wonderful compilation, but today it is a free on-line encyclopedia, as is *The Handbook of African American Texas*. No Texas library would be complete without the latest edition of *The Texas Almanac*, published every two years by TSHA, and *The Handbook of Texas Music*, last updated in 2012, is still available as a printed book.

How much would it cost to buy all 101 books we recommend? Of course, that depends on whether you prefer hardbacks or paperbacks, and which edition is still available. But a rough estimate, choosing paperbacks when possible, would put the figure at around $2,000 to $2,200.

Finally, a word about the qualifications of the two creators of this volume. Each of us has been involved in Texas literary and journalistic endeavors for half a century and we have come to know a good many writers, editors, and publishers on the Texas literary scene. We've both written books about Texas (none of them are included in our listing) and we have read, reviewed, promoted, collected, and generally enjoyed books about Texas all of our adult lives. In that vein, we offer this list of *101 Essential Texas Books* for your consideration.

*Glenn Dromgoole and Carlton Stowers*

# HISTORY

We Texans are proud of a lot of things, but especially our rich and colorful history.

Included in this section are sixteen titles that we believe constitute a literary quilt of the Texas story, from before the Alamo into the twenty-first century, and from a variety of angles, perspectives, styles, cultures, and interests.

Taken together, we hope the books highlighted here offer a starting point for deepening your understanding of, and appreciation for, our distinctive Texas heritage.

# Lone Star
## *A History of Texas and the Texans*

### T. R. Fehrenbach

Macmillan Publishing, 1968; Da Capo Press, 2000

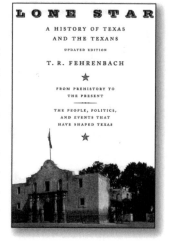

A Midwestern journalist who had just taken a job with a Dallas newspaper asked the best and quickest way to become acquainted with the new state in which he would be working. Read T. R. Fehrenbach's *Lone Star*, he was told.

Such is the lofty position the book enjoys among Texas histories. With a crisp, non-academic writing style, the author offers up a recollection of a land and its people that ranks as the go-to source for those wishing to chart the state's growth. Fehrenbach takes the reader back to a pre-civilization time before there was even a Republic. As a signal of the depth with which he approaches his subject, Fehrenbach opens his first chapter with these words: "In the beginning, before any people, was the land . . . rising out of the warm muck of the green Gulf of Mexico."

It's all here, from the early visiting Spaniards to the Native American tribes, the battles at the Alamo and Goliad to the assassination of President Kennedy. Both praising and unapologetic, *Lone Star* offers insight into the ever-changing attitudes of those who settled the vast region, their politics and faiths, triumphs and shortcomings. And in 750 fast-moving pages the reader meets a remarkable cast of sinners and saints and sees Texas' growth sped along by cattle, cotton, and oil.

In a foreword to an expanded edition of his classic, the author described his intent to write a "general history," free of cumbersome footnotes and scholarly rhetoric. He succeeded admirably.

Another acclaimed comprehensive history of Texas is Randolph B. Campbell's *Gone to Texas* (Oxford University Press, 2003; second edition, 2012).

# ★ Lone Star Nation

*The Epic Story of the Battle for Texas Independence*

## H. W. Brands

Anchor Books, 2005

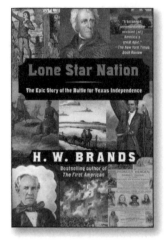

The defining measure of valued historical writing is found not only in its ability to avoid the shortcuts of myth and detours into conjecture but to tell an honest story that offers the quality, pace, and characterization of a well-written novel.

That's what H. W. Brands does in his epic tale of Texas' ongoing battle for independence. Little wonder that he has been a finalist for both the Pulitzer Prize and the *Los Angeles Times* Book Award and reviewers have used words like "masterful" and "extraordinary" to describe *Lone Star Nation*.

While it is obvious that his research of the tumultuous times that led from Spanish exploration to statehood for Texas was exhaustive, it is his exceptional gift of description and portrayal of people and place that sets the book apart.

Breaking the story into time frames, beginning in the late 1700s and carrying it along through 1865, he introduces a cast of fascinating characters ranging from mercenary settlers like Moses and Stephen Austin to those who fought heroically in battles at San Antonio de Bexar and Goliad as well as rival forces, like Antonio Lopez de Santa Anna and his army, who fought mightily to preserve their own empire.

Brands offers new perspective as he explores both the logic and lunacy of taming a vast frontier that was as hostile and unforgiving as it was alluring. In a fair-handed, balanced account he states everyone's case—Indians, Mexicans, settlers, and politicians—and in doing so has produced a revealing re-creation of an important time in not only Texas, but American, history.

# ★ Texian Iliad

*A Military History of the Texas Revolution*

## Stephen L. Hardin

University of Texas Press, 1994

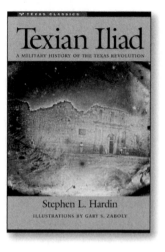

The title for Hardin's award-winning history comes from the observation of a French visitor who listened to the bigger-than-life tales of the Texas Revolution and called it a "Texian Iliad." In his recreation of the battles fought during the march toward statehood and freedom from Mexico's rule, the author examines each of the key events that occurred before and after the legendary and oft-chronicled battle of the Alamo—from the 1824 overthrow of the constitutional government by Santa Anna to his capture at San Jacinto.

And while the events at the Alamo and San Jacinto are given their proper due, Hardin does not overlook lesser-known events that were played out in Gonzales, Goliad, and Conception or the contribution of military leaders whose names are not well known.

Hardin doesn't shy away from pointing out the glaring mistakes and foolish plans designed and carried out by leaders on both sides of the conflict. *Texian Iliad* not only re-introduces the familiar players you've read about in history class but provides detailed accounts of military planning by lesser-knowns like Mexican General Jose Urrea.

Filled with illustrations, photographs, and maps, the book leaves no research avenue unexplored, all the while avoiding the historian's trap of writing strictly for an academic audience. This is Texas history for everyone.

# The Blood of Heroes
*The 13-Day Struggle for the Alamo—*
*and the Sacrifice That Forged a Nation*

**James Donovan**

Little, Brown, 2012

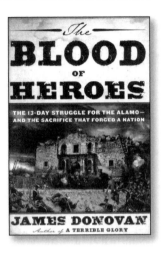

It is safe to say that if all the books written on the battle of the Alamo were placed end to end, they would reach from here to San Antonio de Bexar. No single event defines Texas history as does the thirteen-day siege in 1836 wherein the likes of William Barrett Travis, Jim Bowie, and Davy Crockett held off almost 2,000 Mexican soldiers under the command of Antonio Lopez de Santa Anna before falling to glorious defeat.

Written with a keen eye for detail, a fast-paced writing style, and a scholar's devotion to research, James Donovan's *The Blood of Heroes* has been hailed by many reviewers and historians as the definitive book on the subject—providing minute-by-minute detail to the days leading up to the attack, the siege and its aftermath, and also personalizing those involved. The reader gains an understanding of why and how the bloody event occurred and comes to know the principals, from the power-mad Santa Anna to the colorful and courageous Alamo defenders.

Donovan, from his research, offers his answers to questions that have long lingered: Did Crockett die in the heat of battle or was he executed after the mission was taken? Did Travis actually draw the line in the sand, asking those willing to give their lives for the cause to step across?

Even for those who have read such applauded accounts as Walter Lord's *A Time to Stand* and Lon Tinkle's *13 Days to Glory*, this is a fresh and insightful look at the signature event in Texas history.

# ☆ Texas Flags

## Robert Maberry Jr.

Texas A&M University Press, 2002

Ask most Texans how many flags have flown over the Lone Star State, and they will probably say six. We've all been to Six Flags Over Texas, after all.

But as this full-color, coffee-table volume illustrates, more than a hundred different flags have actually flown in Texas. There wasn't just one Texas, or Texian, flag but several. The same with Mexican flags, Confederate flags, U.S. flags. There were Texas Ranger flags, cavalry flags, and division flags from World Wars I and II and the Spanish-American War.

With 117 color illustrations, including thirty-two full-page reproductions of various flags, Maberry documents the colorful history of flags in Texas and the myths, stories, and facts associated with the various banners. The book was written initially to accompany an exhibition at the Museum of Fine Arts in Houston.

Another colorful book about Texas flags is Alan K. Sumrall's *Battle Flags of Texans in the Confederacy* (Eakin Press, 1995), documenting more than sixty regimental flags and the stories behind them.

# Texas and Texans in the Civil War

## Ralph A. Wooster

Eakin Press, 1995

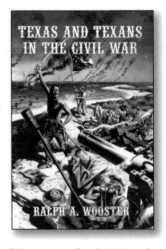

Numerous books have been written on the Civil War in Texas, or the role Texans played in battles outside the state, most of them concentrating on one particular campaign, or one unit, or one soldier or officer's story, or one aspect of the war. In *Texas and Texans in the Civil War*, Ralph Wooster provides an overview of the subject, from secession to reconstruction.

"Although a frontier state spared the devastation that took place in Virginia, Tennessee, and Georgia," Wooster writes, "Texas nevertheless played a major role in the Civil War. The last battle of the war was fought in South Texas a month after Lee surrendered at Appomattox (and) Texans were involved in almost every great battle of the war."

Wooster divides his account into seven chapters: secession; early phases of the war (1861–62); the war comes to Texas (1862–63); life on the home front; the end draws near (1864); defeat of the Confederacy; and aftermath. He tells the story in about 200 pages, with an additional hundred pages of notes, bibliography, and index—a scholarly yet readable approach.

Wooster also wrote a condensed version (eighty-eight pages)—*Civil War Texas: A History and a Guide*—for the Fred Rider Cotten Popular History Series published by the Texas State Historical Association.

Thomas E. Alexander and Dan K. Utley compiled *Go Where the Fighting Was Fiercest: The Guide to the Texas Civil War Monuments* (State House, 2013), showing where Texans fought and died in the war and the plaques acknowledging their sacrifices, from Shiloh to Gettysburg. Kelly McMichael's *Sacred Memories: The Civil War Monument Movement in Texas* (TSHA, 2009) offers an in-state tour of Civil War memorials.

# Empire of the Summer Moon

*Quanah Parker and the Rise and Fall of the Comanches, the Most Powerful Indian Tribe in American History*

## S. C. Gwynne

Scribner, 2010

Few social changes in Texas history rival the rise and fall of the equally proud and violent Comanche nation, and author S. C. Gwynne's brutal and compelling account stands as the definitive work on the subject. A finalist for the Pulitzer Prize, the book tells the story of the tribe's triumphs and tragedies, its glory days, and its ultimate defeat at the hands of military Indian hunters.

The reader not only learns of the hard-fought settling of the Texas plains, meeting remarkable characters like legendary chief Quanah Parker and his chief adversary, Colonel Ranald Slidell Mackenzie, commander of the 4th U.S. Calvary, but gets an eventful view of the Comanche culture. And, of course, there's Cynthia Ann Parker, the famed white captive who ultimately married into the tribe.

From buffalo hunts to bloodthirsty raids, Gwynne's book is a finely researched account of a people who were proud, oppressed, and immorally savage. This is Texas history as it should be told, bold and honest, with all its color and brutality intact.

For more on the subject, consider *The Captured* by Scott Zesch, *The Comanche Empire* by Pekka Hamalainen, *The Searchers: The Making of an American Legend* by Glenn Frankel, and two classics back in print, *The Comanche Barrier to South Plains Settlement* by Rupert N. Richardson and *Indian Depredations in Texas* by J. W. Wilbarger.

# Buffalo Guns & Barbed Wire

## Don Hampton Biggers

Texas Tech University Press, 1991

*Buffalo Guns & Barbed* Wire is a combined reissue of two books by frontier newspaperman Don Hampton Biggers, who interviewed a number of old buffalo hunters and early cattlemen and wrote their stories in *History That Will Never Be Repeated* (1901) and *Pictures of the Past* (1902). The handsome reissued volume from Texas Tech Press includes an introduction by A. C. Greene and a biography of Biggers by Seymour V. Connor.

Greene said Biggers "catches the flavor and the intent of those he interviewed out on the old buffalo range, in the sudden-like towns, on the vast ranches. He may glorify their exploits a shade too enthusiastically, but he never worships them, and he tells their stories warts and all."

His two original books were published under the pen name Lan Franks and are extremely rare. *History That Will Never Be Repeated* concerns early-day cattle and ranching history. *Pictures of the Past* deals with the buffalo slaughter, and Greene said it was more valuable "simply because it gives us the kind of information available nowhere else."

The volumes, Greene noted, contained factual and spelling errors but "on the whole, Biggers' works are downright scholarly to be coming out of a small West Texas cattle town." In the reissued book, the buffalo hunting stories are presented first, then the ranching stories.

*Buffalo Guns & Barbed Wire* also includes historic photographs by George Robertson (on buffalo hunting) and Erwin E. Smith (on early ranching).

# ⭐ Sketches from the Five States of Texas

## A. C. Greene

Texas A&M University Press, 1998

When Texas was annexed into the United States in 1845, it retained the right to voluntarily divide itself into five separate states. That hasn't happened, of course, but the state does fall naturally into five geographically distinct regions— North Texas, South Texas, East Texas, West Texas, and Central Texas.

For several years noted Texas author and historian A. C. Greene wrote a series of Texas sketches for the *Dallas Morning News,* and those pieces constitute the bulk of *Sketches from the Five States of Texas.* The collection includes more than a hundred one- to two-page stories about interesting Texas events, facts, and personalities, with about twenty pieces under each of the five "states."

A few examples: "The First Black Millionaire" (East Texas), "Last Shot of the Civil War" (South Texas), "Socialist Songster" (North Texas), "Lockhart's Lovely Library" (Central Texas), and "Texas' First Fire Truck" (West Texas). Each story can be read in five minutes or less and, taken together, they offer a lot of Texas history probably not familiar to most readers.

*Texas Stories I Like to Tell My Friends* and *More Texas Stories* by historian T. Lindsay Baker (ACU Press, 2011–12) comprise about 200 short pieces about Texas history odds and ends. The first book focuses on the nineteenth century, the second on the twentieth century.

Another good collection is *It Happened in Texas* by James A. Crutchfield (Two Dot), consisting of thirty-four interesting episodes from Texas history.

#  Twentieth-Century Texas:
## *A Social and Cultural History*

### Edited by John W. Storey and Mary L. Kelley

University of North Texas Press, 2008

Here is a book on Texas history that takes up where a lot of books leave off. *Twentieth-Century Texas* covers the enormous changes that Texas went through from 1900 to 2000.

Edited by history professors John W. Storey and Mary L. Kelley, the 480- page volume includes fifteen historical essays by different Texas writers and covering a number of topics rarely dwelled on in Texas history books.

Texas State Historian Bill O'Neal, for example, has a twenty-two page piece on the history of sports in Texas, while professor/ critic Don Graham takes a look at Texas in the movies, music historian Gary Hartman writes about women and gender in Texas music, and Ralph Wooster considers the effects that war had on Texas society and culture in the 1900s.

In "Pagodas Amid the Steeples: The Changing Religious Landscape," Storey points out that by the end of the twentieth century Catholics had overtaken Baptists as the state's largest religious group, and church steeples "now shared the urban skyline with pagodas, mosques, mandirs, gurdwaras, and synagogues."

The volume opens with four essays covering the changes affecting Indians, Mexican Americans, African Americans, and women in Texas. Other chapters look at literature, art, philanthropy, public schools, the environment, and science and technology.

At the conclusion of each essay are endnotes and suggestions for further reading. *Twentieth-Century Texas* fills some gaps in the literature about Texas history.

# ⭐ Texas Post Office Murals
*Art for the People*

## Philip Parisi

Texas A&M University Press, 2004

**During the Depression,** the Section of Fine Arts commissioned murals at sixty-nine post offices and federal buildings in Texas as a way of giving work to artists and offering a little hope and beauty to people who were seeing very little of either in the 1930s.

In his full-color book, Philip Parisi gathered 115 photographs of these historic works of art and tells the stories of how they came to be, how they affected their communities, and what efforts have been made to preserve them.

The paintings by such artists as Tom Lea, Jerry Bywaters, Peter Hurd, Alexandre Hogue, and Xavier Gonzalez depicted colorful scenes and subject matter that people could relate to. A good many of the Texas scenes, for example, featured cattle, buffalo, horses, and Indians. Some showed people at work at industries specific to the region, or community symbols like Eastland's legendary horned toad Ol' Rip.

The murals are presented alphabetically by city. A color picture of each mural is shown accompanied by a short narrative about the artwork, the name of the artist and how much he or she was paid, the location of the building, and the condition of the mural today. Most, surprisingly, are still in good condition. A few have been destroyed or are not available for public viewing.

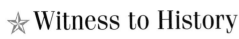# Witness to History
*November 22, 1963*

## Hugh Aynesworth

Brown Books Publishing Group, 2013

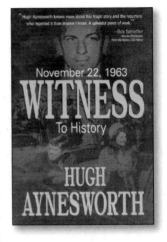

The great irony imbedded in four-time Pulitzer Prize finalist Hugh Aynesworth's involvement in coverage of the assassination of President John Kennedy lies in the fact he was one of the few front line *Dallas Morning News* reporters *not* assigned to cover any aspect of the presidential visit on that November day in 1963.

A young aviation and space program reporter at the time, he had nonetheless decided to slip away and join the crowds gathered to watch the presidential motorcade pass. It was a decision that would be the first step toward recognition as one of the leading experts on the tragic event and its lingering aftermath. Before all was said and done, Aynesworth had not only been an eyewitness to the assassination of Kennedy, but was in the Texas Theater later in the day when accused killer Lee Harvey Oswald was arrested, then saw Dallas nightclub owner Jack Ruby shoot and kill Oswald in the basement of the Dallas Police Department.

In short order he became one of the country's leading experts on the historic tragedy. It was Aynesworth who received Oswald's infamous "Russian diary," and to whom members of Ruby's family confided and even asked that he serve as a pallbearer at Ruby's funeral (an invitation he declined).

His highly personal look at reporting the case for a half century not only offers a unique vantage point from which to view the oft-told story but is a candid and revealing look at how investigative journalism is practiced. Oswald's mother Marguerite and wife Marina, law enforcement officials, conspiracy mongers, and fellow journalists all come to life in *Witness to History*.

# ⭐ Texas Political Memorabilia

*Buttons, Bumper Stickers, and Broadsides*

## Chuck Bailey with Bill Crawford

University of Texas Press, 2007

Chuck Bailey was in the sixth grade in 1960 when his father gave him a sack of Kennedy-Johnson buttons. As one of just two Kennedy-Johnson supporters in his class, Bailey said he was glad to get the buttons. An avid collector of baseball cards, comic books, pennants, coins, and rocks, Bailey soon found himself collecting political memorabilia.

Nearly fifty years later he shared his collection with readers in *Texas Political Memorabilia*. Each two-page spread in the book includes a page of color photographs of various political buttons and gadgets, with an identification and explanation on the opposite page.

As longtime *Texas Monthly* political observer Paul Burka noted, Bailey "has found a new way to tell the history of Texas politics." The book begins with presidential items from the campaigns of Lyndon Johnson and the two George Bushes, followed by memorabilia from U.S. Senate and U.S. House of Representative races in Texas, campaigns for governor, and other state offices, even some local elections.

In addition to buttons and bumper stickers, Bailey has collected all sorts of items used in political campaigns—matchbooks, playing cards, ties, golf tees, hair clips, pocket knives, even shoelaces, chewing gum, peanuts, and pickles.

Readers will find themselves drawn into the campaigns, reminiscing about some of the iconic Texas political figures, and wanting to read more about others.

#  Texans All Series

## Sara R. Massey, General Editor

The Mexican Texans by Phyllis McKenzie
The Indian Texans by James M. Smallwood
The African Texans by Alwyn Barr
The Asian Texans by Marilyn Dell Brady
The European Texans by Allan O. Kownslar

Texas A&M University Press, 2004

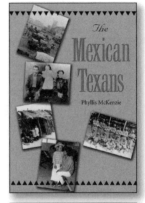

The Institute of Texan Cultures and Texas A&M University Press teamed up to produce an impressive and engaging five-book series exploring and celebrating the contributions, history, traditions, and culture of five principal cultural groups in Texas.

Five different authors wrote the accounts, drawing on their own research as well as the extensive collection at the Institute of Texan Cultures in San Antonio. What emerged were five well-written, heavily-illustrated, reasonably-priced, and quite approachable histories intended for school and public libraries as well as homes. The books were designed to appeal to middle school students studying Texas history, but adult readers will also find them interesting and informative.

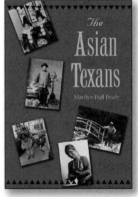

Each book, distinctive in writing style and tone, is 140–160 pages. Together, they provide a compelling portrait of the rich diversity of Texas history and culture. The series is considered here as one entry in our list of *101 Essential Texas Books*.

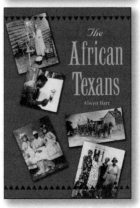

# Texas Through Women's Eyes

## The Twentieth Century Experience

### Judith N. McArthur and Harold L. Smith

University of Texas Press, 2010

*Texas Through Women's Eyes* tells the social history of Texas women in the twentieth century. The authors felt that women had not been given proper attention in history books. Their book "grew out of our frustration with the inadequate discussion of women in Texas history survey texts. We were especially disturbed by the lengthy silences regarding women's experiences between 1900 and 2000."

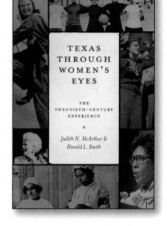

They divide their book into four eras: 1900–1920, 1920–1945, 1945–1965, and 1965–2000.

Within each section are two- to four-page discussions of a variety of topics and issues related to women's lives.

For example, Part Three covers 1945–1965 and deals primarily with Conformity, Civil Rights, and Social Protest. Under that section are these topics: gender roles and the domestic ideal; women at work; civil rights (brown and black); red scare politics and the Minute Women; women and the rise of the Republican Party; and legal rights.

Of special interest is the documents appendix at the end of each section—first person articles, letters, and oral histories by Texas women about their own experiences or points of view. At the end of Part Four, for example, are several articles debating women's rights from a variety of viewpoints, as well as pieces by Barbara Jordan and Ann Richards on how they got into politics and by Jennifer Chau on being Vietnamese and Texan.

*Texas Through Women's Eyes* is a thorough, important, and compelling addition to the literature dealing with modern Texas history.

# The History of Texas Music

### Gary Hartman

Texas A&M University Press, 2008

The diversity of Texas music is celebrated in *The History of Texas Music* by Gary Hartman, founding director of the Center for Texas Music History at Texas State University.

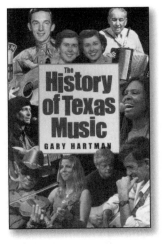

"Although many people may think of country music when they think of the Lone Star State," writes Hartman, "Texas actually encompasses a wide variety of ethnic musical genres and regional styles."

Among them are German, Czech, Tejano, Cajun, rock and roll, rhythm and blues, and Western swing. Hartman discusses the history and culture of each musical style, liberally illustrating his text with black and white photos of Texas musicians past and present—Willie Nelson, George Strait, Roy Orbison, ZZ Top, Mance Lipscomb, and many more.

Separate chapters explore the history of the various musical styles, and at the end of each chapter Hartman includes a recommended listening list of fifteen to twenty artists and their albums. He also includes an extensive bibliography and endnotes for those inclined to go into more depth.

Another important work is *The Roots of Texas Music,* edited by Lawrence Clayton and Joe Specht (A&M, 2003), which focuses on the contributions of Texas musicians from 1900 to 1950. And *The Handbook of Texas Music* from the Texas State Historical Association is a comprehensive encyclopedic reference.

For a fascinating view of the explosion of the Austin music scene in the early '70s, read Jan Reid's *The Improbable Rise of Redneck Rock.* Published in 1974 and updated in 2004 (UT Press), the book traces the careers of Willie Nelson, Janis Joplin, Billie Joe Shaver, Kinky Friedman, Marcia Ball, and others.

# Some Other Notable Titles

⭐ *The Great Plains,* Walter Prescott Webb's sweeping southwest history published in 1932 (reprinted by University of Nebraska Press), remains an important work for modern-day authors wishing to learn more about the region's settlement history, geography, climate, demographics, and mindsets.

⭐ *Texas: A Historical Atlas* by A. Ray Stephens, cartography by Carol Zuber-Mallison (Oklahoma, 2010) is a nine-by-twelve, 400-page collection of eighty-six essays and 175 full-color maps on Texas history and geography. Besides its value as a historical resource, it makes a good impression on a bookshelf or coffee table.

⭐ *The Alamo and Beyond: A Collector's Journey* by international rock star Phil Collins (State House, 2012) is a 400-page, full-color coffee-table book displaying the musician's incredible private collection of Alamo documents and artifacts, resulting from his lifelong fascination with Davy Crockett and the Alamo.

⭐ *Three Roads to the Alamo* is William C. Davis's acclaimed account of the lives of Crockett, Bowie, and Travis, the historical forces that brought them together, and what happened at the Alamo (HarperCollins, 1998).

⭐ *Women and the Texas Revolution,* edited by Mary L. Scheer (North Texas, 2012) is a collection of eight scholarly essays dealing in depth with such topics as Hispanic women on the losing side of the Texas revolution, black women and the revolution, and women at the Alamo, the runaway scrape, and San Jacinto.

⭐ B. P. Gallaway's *The Ragged Rebel: A Common Soldier in W.H. Parsons' Texas Cavalry, 1861–1865* (UT, 1988; ACU Press, 2010) tells the riveting story of one young man's Civil War experiences in Texas, Louisiana, and Arkansas. He was shot in the neck, captured, and severely burned in a gunpowder plant explosion, yet lived to tell his story.

⭐ *Historic Texas from the Air* by Gerald Saxon, David Buisserer, Richard Francaviglia and photos by Jack W. Graves Jr. (UT, 2009) is a colorful and informative coffee table book that focuses on seventy-three historic sites. Graves' aerial photographs are the highlight of the book, but each photo is accompanied by a page or two of text explaining the site's significance.

⭐ It's not a Texas book per se, but *Escape from Davao* by John Lukacs (Simon & Schuster, 2010) features a Texan throughout—Edwin Dyess, for whom Dyess Air Force Base in Abilene is named. The book details the horrendous suffering of American POWs in the Philippines during World War II and the daring escape of ten of them from a Japanese prison camp. See also *Bataan Death March: A Survivor's Account* by Edwin Dyess, published in 1944 and back in print (Bison Books).

⭐ *Black Women in Texas History,* edited by Bruce Glasrud and Merline Pitre (A&M, 2008), includes eight essays tracing the experiences and contributions of black women chronologically from slavery days to the modern era.

⭐ Sean P. Cunningham details how Texas went from essentially being a one-party state controlled by conservative Democrats to a one-party state controlled by conservative Republicans in *Cowboy Conservatism: Texas and the Rise of the Modern Right* (University Press of Kentucky, 2010).

⭐ *West Texas: A History of the Giant Side of the State*, edited by Paul H. Carlson and Bruce A. Glasrud (University of Oklahoma Press, 2014) explores the region's history from a variety of perspectives and viewpoints. Eighteen historians contributed essays to the collection, which is divided into four sections: The Place, The People, Political and Economic Life, and Society and Culture.

# LITERATURE

For decades public school students in Texas have been required to take courses in Texas history, and generations of Texans have grown up knowing at least as much about their state's history as their nation's history.

Perhaps it is time for students—at whatever age—to be given instruction in Texas literature as well, offering a sampling of stories, poems, essays, and novels from Texas writers past and present.

The selections in this section would be a good place to start.

# 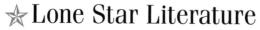 Lone Star Literature
*From the Red River to the Rio Grande*

### Edited by Don Graham

W. W. Norton & Co., 2003, 2006

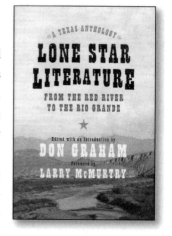

**Don Graham, longtime** teacher and critic of Texas and Southwest literature, focuses on a century of Texas writing, from 1903 to 2002, beginning with stories and essays that dealt with the frontier and concluding with contemporary writers covering urban themes.

Although Graham excludes poetry from the book, his anthology serves as an excellent representative sampling of top Texas writers, with sixty-three pieces by such writers as John Lomax, O. Henry, Sallie Reynolds Matthews, Walter Prescott Webb, Dorothy Scarborough, J. Frank Dobie, A. C. Greene, John Graves, Katherine Anne Porter, George Sessions Perry, Bill Brett, Américo Paredes, Elmer Kelton, Sandra Cisneros, Shelby Hearon, Naomi Shihab Nye, Mary Karr, Larry L. King, and Molly Ivins. Larry McMurtry, represented in the book with an excerpt from *The Last Picture Show*, wrote a brief foreword noting there is "much to enjoy" in the collection.

Graham said the anthology "seeks to provide through fiction, autobiography, and a few discursive essays an overview of the diversity, excellence, and characteristic tropes of Texas writing." *Lone Star Literature* should be appreciated by serious students of Texas letters—or by anyone who just likes to settle in and read some good stories.

# I'll Tell You a Tale

*An Anthology*

## J. Frank Dobie

Little, Brown, 1960; University of Texas Press, 1981

J. Frank Dobie (1888–1964) was Texas' best-known, most nationally recognized writer in the first half of the twentieth century, and his reputation as a masterful teller of tales survives fifty years after his death.

He is credited with helping save the breed of Texas Longhorns from extinction and for promoting Texas folklore through books and publications he edited for the Texas Folklore Society. Four days before his death, Dobie was awarded the nation's highest civilian award, the Medal of Freedom, by President Lyndon B. Johnson.

*I'll Tell You a Tale* is an anthology drawn from Dobie's writing, including *The Longhorns*, *The Mustangs*, *Tales of Old-Time Texas*, *Coronado's Children*, and *Apache Gold and Yaqui Silver.* All of those books, and others, remain in print as part of UT Press's Dobie collection.

The anthology was put together by Isabel Gaddis, one of Dobie's former students at the University of Texas, where he created and taught the course "Life and Literature of the Southwest" for many years. Dobie approved the selections and even rewrote a few of the stories for the book.

For more about Dobie, see *J. Frank Dobie: A Liberated Mind* by Steven L. Davis, and *Three Friends: Roy Bedichek, J. Frank Dobie, Walter Prescott Webb* by William A. Owens (both from UT Press).

#  Literary Fort Worth (2002)

Judy Alter and James Ward Lee, Editors

## Literary Austin (2007)

Don Graham, Editor

## Literary Dallas (2008)

Frances Brannen Vick, Editor

## Literary El Paso (2009)

Marcia Hatfield Daudistel, Editor

## Literary Houston (2011)

David Theis, Editor

Published by TCU Press

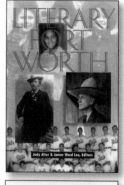

The literary cities series from TCU Press began with *Literary Fort Worth* before moving on to volumes on Austin, Dallas, El Paso, and Houston, with one on San Antonio still to come. Each volume includes dozens of pieces—fiction, non-fiction, poetry—by indigenous writers as well as visiting observers who wrote about the city.

The impressive list of contributors to each volume is reason enough for a Texas reader to want to peruse all six books. The Austin book, in particular, reads like a who's who in Texas letters, with pieces by O. Henry, J. Frank Dobie, Willie Morris, Larry McMurtry, A. C. Greene, Liz Carpenter, Don Graham, Ronnie Dugger, Stephen Harrigan, Molly Ivins, Kinky Friedman, and Prudence Macintosh, among others. Each collection features familiar writers well known locally and regionally, with extensive author bios.

The Fort Worth book is arranged alphabetically by writer, while the other volumes are presented chronologically or thematically.

# ⭐ Texas in Poetry 2

## Billy Bob Hill

TCU Press, 2002

*Texas in Poetry 2* is a revised and expanded edition of Billy Bob Hill's earlier work, *Texas in Poetry: A 150-Year Anthology,* now out of print. The impressive volume includes more than 360 poems by more than 150 Texas poets. Hill includes a brief biographical listing for each poet.

In selecting the poems to include, Hill went to great effort to see that the book is representative of the styles, themes, perspectives, and backgrounds of Texas poets from the state's revolutionary era to today. They include Sam Houston's 1835 lyrical battle cry, "Texian Call to Arms," and Margaret Lea Houston's 1844 tribute, "To My Husband."

Grace Noll Crowell, who achieved national recognition as a Texas poet, is represented by "A Prayer for Texas" (1936) and two others. Quite a few other Texas poet laureates—some who achieved that status even after *Texas in Poetry 2* was published in 2002—have verses in the book.

Popular Texas writers Walt McDonald, Robert James Waller, Sandra Cisneros, Naomi Shihab Nye, Robert A. Fink, Larry D. Thomas, Benjamin Saenz, Paul Ruffin, James Hoggard, Stephen Harrigan, and the late A. C. Greene are represented. Classic poems include Bonnie Parker's "The Story of Bonnie and Clyde," W. Lee O'Daniel's "Beautiful Texas," and Lawrence Chittenden's "The Cowboys' Christmas Ball."

Hill also produced *A Students' Treasury of Texas Poetry* (TCU, 2007) intended for high school readers.

# Notes from Texas

*On Writing in the Lone Star State*

**Edited by W. C. Jameson**

TCU Press, 2008

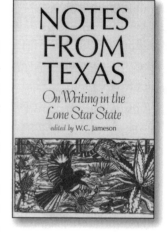

Fourteen contemporary Texas authors contributed thoughtful essays about writing—and how Texas influenced their writing—in this collection that could serve as a primer for aspiring writers seeking to understand the craft. Or just a delightful anthology of good writing by good writers on the subject of writing.

Most of the pieces are fifteen to twenty pages in length, meant to be read and savored one essay at a time. Although the theme, approach, and style of the articles vary from writer to writer, each piece can be read in thirty minutes or so. Together, they provide an appreciation of the richness and the diversity of the literary landscape of Texas.

The authors' expositions are presented in alphabetical order, and it's quite a lineup: Judy Alter, Robert Flynn, Don Graham, Rolando Hinojosa-Smith, Paulette Jiles, Elmer Kelton, Larry L. King, James Ward Lee, James Reasoner, Clay Reynolds, Joyce Gibson Roach, Red Steagall, Carlton Stowers, and Frances Brannen Vick.

Readers who might not be familiar with all of the names are encouraged to use the essays as a springboard to delving more deeply into their work.

 # Let's Hear It

*Stories by Texas Women Writers*

## Edited by Sylvia Ann Grider and
## Lou Halsell Rodenberger

Texas A&M University Press, 2003

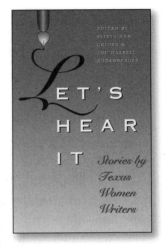

*Let's Hear It* includes twenty-two short stories by Texas women writers from the Civil War to modern days. The collection is divided chronologically into four eras: Civil War to early 1900s, 1920-1950s, 1960-1980s, and the 1990s.

The twenty-two writers are introduced with brief essays, followed by a representative short story from each writer, covering a variety of themes and topics. In an introductory essay, the editors credit Katherine Anne Porter as "the most distinguished of the many Texas writers of short fiction who later followed her lead." Porter was awarded the Pulitzer Prize in 1966 for *The Collected Stories of Katherine Anne Porter*. One of those stories, "The Circus," is included in *Let's Hear It*.

Other writers represented are Aurelia Hadley Mohl, Belle Hunt Shortridge, Mollie E. Moore Davis, Olive Huck, Dorothy Scarborough, Winifred Sanford, Margaret Cousins, Loula Grace Erdman, Jane Gilmore Rushing, Beverly Lowry, Carolyn Osborn, Laverne Harrell Clark, and Annette Sanford. Modern era writers include Joyce Gibson Roach, Sunny Nash, Denisse Chavez, Susan Ford Wiltshire, Betty Wiesepape, Judy Alter, Jan Epton Seale, and Jill Patterson.

Editors Sylvia Ann Grider and Lou Halsell Rodenberger also teamed up to produce a collection of biographical essays, *Texas Women Writers: A Tradition of Their Own* (Texas A&M, 1997).

# 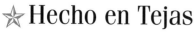 Hecho en Tejas
*An Anthology of Texas Mexican Literature*

## Edited by Dagoberto Gilb

University of New Mexico Press, 2006

*Hecho en Tejas* is an impressive and unrivaled 528-page collection of more than a hundred poems, song lyrics, stories, and essays by Tejano writers over the years.

The anthology begins with an account by Alvar Nuñez Cabeza de Vaca from 1528 and includes mostly poems and songs—and some photographs—through the 1940s. But beginning in the '50s, and especially with Américo Paredes, writers were expressing themselves through prose as well as verse, and by the 1970s and '80s there was an explosion of Tejano talent being published— José Angel Gutiérrez, Roy Benavidez, Rolando Hinojosa-Smith, Max Martinez, Lionel G. Garcia, Sandra Cisneros, Dagoberto Gilb, Pat Mora, Tish Hinojosa, and many more.

The entries are arranged chronologically by decade, with the bulk of the pieces from the 1970s forward, including a dozen writers who have made a name for themselves since the turn of the century.

While it is a scholarly effort worthy of high school and college literature study, editor Gilb noted that he hoped the collection would also "reach everyday readers of all kinds who love Texas . . . a book that so many can learn from, both the young who don't know and the old who do but want it remembered, both those inside the culture and outside."

# In a Special Light

**Elroy Bode**

Trinity University Press, 2006

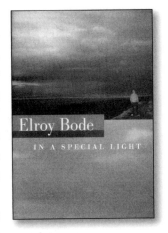

Some writers defy literary classification, aside from having fine-tuned a reputation as master craftsmen. Elroy Bode, a lifelong observer of all things Texan, calls most of the short pieces he has produced over the past forty years "sketches." Those a bit more highbrow might refer to them as highly personal essays. Simply put, they are a man's thoughts on and reaction to those things that have affected his life.

From the Hill Country to the border regions of far West Texas, he has chronicled his encounters with simple pleasures—music, wildlife, old friends, and solitary walks—and poignant moments—the death of a beloved son and the passing of old traditions. Whatever his subject, Bode always treats it with an honest and lyrical touch.

Readers of *In a Special Light*, the ninth collection of his career, become intimately familiar with the sights and sounds of his homeland. We've all seen many of the same things Bode has, had many similar experiences, yet few have his rare gift for so eloquently sharing them with others.

A public school teacher for forty-eight years, Bode has never sought the bright lights of literary commerce. Still, he has been unable to avoid recognition—the Spur Award from the Western Writers of America for his short fiction, the Stanley Walker Award for Journalism from the Texas Institute of Letters, twice. Though long retired from the classroom, he teaches still.

# Curmudgeon in Corduroy

## The Best of Jerry Flemmons' Texas

TCU Press, 2000

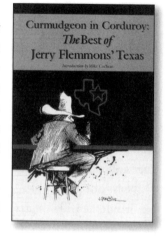

Jerry Flemmons, a columnist for the *Fort Worth Star*-Telegram for most of his career, was one of the best writers in the rich history of Texas journalism. This collection of thirty-eight essays was published the year after he died in 1999. Although Flemmons traversed the world as the newspaper's travel editor, he never wandered far from his West Texas roots, as these pieces illustrate.

Flemmons rhapsodizes about some favorite Texas foods—chicken-fried steak, black-eyed peas, cornbread, Frito pie—small town living, courthouse squares, front porches, cutting horses, cowboy hats, the domino game 42, the hymn "Amazing Grace," the Texas two-step, West Texas football, West Texas women, and the mesquite tree.

An uncommon observer of common things, Flemmons wrote eloquently about simplicity. He loved words, studied them, devoured them, and in the end enriched them and graced them and gave life to them through his writing. He painted pictures with them.

Flemmons, a voracious reader, also sifted through old books and periodicals to glean hundreds of tidbits about Texas history and lore—from the serious to the ridiculous. His two collections, *Texas Siftings* and *More Texas Siftings* (TCU Press), contain such gems as Charlie Goodnight explaining how to eat prairie dogs, an 1848 Texas Christmas dinner menu, a partial list of Kansas ladies who greeted Texas cowboys at the end of a trail drive, a recipe for jackrabbit in mushroom gravy, and the heaviest governor of Texas.

# Texas Literary Outlaws
*Six Writers in the Sixties and Beyond*

## Steven L. Davis

TCU Press, 2004

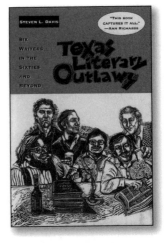

There are those, particularly inhabitants of the "Austin literary community," who insist that the '60s and '70s represented the Golden Age of Texas writers. And it was a group of good buddy journalists-novelists who called themselves the Mad Dogs that commanded the lion's share of attention and adulation.

You had Dan Jenkins, reporting for *Sports Illustrated* and writing bestsellers like *Semi-Tough*; Larry L. King, writing for *Harper's* and giving birth to the Broadway smash, *Best Little Whorehouse in Texas*; and *Texas Monthly* staffer, screenwriter, and novelist Gary Cartwright. Add Bud Shrake (*Strange Peaches, But Not for Love*) , Bill Brammer (*The Gay Place*), and Pete Gent (*North Dallas Forty*), toss in ample amounts of high grade partying, and you've got the makings for a book on the good-timing, cutting edge writing careers which author Davis chronicles.

Though one wonders how they found time to sit and write, there is no doubt that the Mad Dogs were a rarely talented lot, winning lofty awards, climbing bestseller lists, and watching their books made into successful movies. Theirs was a free-wheeling time of rapid social change and New Age mindsets. Not only did they live it to the fullest, they wrote about it with exceptional style and flair.

# Some Other Notable Titles

⭐ *Texas Plays*, edited by William B. Martin (SMU, 1990), is an anthology of nine plays by nine Texas playwrights, including Horton Foote (*A Trip to Bountiful*), Ramsey Yelvington (*A Cloud of Witnesses*), and Preston Jones (*Lu Ann Hampton Laverty Oberlander*). All are set in Texas but represent different forms and styles, with comedy predominating.

⭐ One of Texas' best known essayists and folklorists, James Ward Lee offers a fascinating review of the state's literature and social mores in his *Adventures with a Texas Humanist* (TCU, 2004). From J. Frank Dobie to Larry McMurtry, Lee chronicles the trends, politics, and social changes addressed by Texas writers.

⭐ Three excellent collections of Texas short fiction, edited by Kay Cattarulla, were published by SMU Press from 1994 to 2001 as *Texas Bound* (volumes one, two, and three) and are still in print. Eight stories from the first volume are also available on cassette, read by actors. It is worth digging out the old cassette player just to hear Lynna Williams' story, "Personal Testimony."

⭐ In the introduction to his *Texas Road Trip* (TCU, 2004), Bryan Woolley notes there are 300,000 miles of highways and paved streets in the state. After reading his delightful anecdotes and personal observations, you'll feel you've traveled every mile with him.

⭐ *Talking with Texas Writers: Twelve Interviews* by Patrick Bennett (Texas A&M, 1980) comprises discussions about the subjects' work and about Texas writing in general. The writers interviewed were A. C. Greene, Elmer Kelton, Leon Hale, Frances Mossiker, Larry McMurtry, John Graves, Shelby Hearon, Preston Jones, Max Apple, William Goyen, Larry L. King, and Tom Lea.

⭐ *Conversations with Texas Writers*, edited by Frances Leonard and Ramona Cearley (UT, 2005), includes interviews with fifty writers, but just three who were also interviewed by Bennett twenty-five years earlier—McMurtry, Kelton and Graves. Others in the book include Sarah Bird, Kinky Friedman,

Horton Foote, Elizabeth Crook, Naomi Shihab Nye, Stephen Harrigan, Molly Ivins, Bill Wittliff, and David Lindsey.

☆ For his efforts to bring cowboy poetry to the awareness of the mainstream, gifted musician Red Steagall was named the Official Cowboy Poet of Texas in 1991. And his *Ride for the Brand* (TCU) demonstrates that the title was well-earned. The only thing better that reading Steagall's lyrical poems is hearing him recite them. He was named Texas Poet Laureate in 2006.

☆ The fact that Ben K. Green's classic *Horse Tradin'* (Knopf, 1967; Bison, 1999) remains in print after almost a half century is evidence enough that the veterinarian/horse trader/author knew his subject well. His tales of dealing in the horse trade are filled with folksy yet lyrical prose that gives the book its enduring quality. The same can be said of his *The Village Horse Doctor*.

# Fiction

Time was when there was a snob-bish mindset back East that the only fiction being produced south of the Red River consisted of paperback shoot-'em-ups and endless stories of dusty trail drives.

While authors stubbornly continue to re-visit the Old West—winning Pulitzers for their efforts, by the way—the landscape of Texas fiction has expanded, modernized, even grown sassy and hip. And it gets better with every new publishing season.

Which is, as you'll see by the following recommendations, proof positive that Texas storytelling needs no apology.

# ★ The Time It Never Rained

## Elmer Kelton

Doubleday, 1973; TCU, 1984; Forge, 2008

The task of selecting the best book from Elmer Kelton's remarkable body of work is not easy and is likely to generate considerable argument. This, after all, is the man who received the Western Writers of America's Spur Award for the year's best novel no less than *seven times* during his career. Kelton owned the genre with his keen attention to Old West history, his well-drawn characters, and his fluid writing style.

And while he wrote with an expert's touch of range wars and cattle drives, good guys and bad, he soared to a new level with the closest he ever came to writing a contemporary novel. Set during the seven-year drought of the West Texas 1950s, *The Time It Never Rained* was justifiably called by critic Jon Tuska "one of the dozen or so best novels written by an American in this century."

The story focuses on rancher Charley Flagg as he stubbornly holds to the fast fading ranchers' mindset, refusing government assistance and unwilling to give in to nature's harsh treatment. Through Flagg's eyes we see a fast-changing world that he's unwilling to give in to. Whether this book's your absolute favorite or not, it is hard to argue that Kelton ever fashioned a more memorable character than Flagg.

Unless, that is, you want to toss cowboy Hewey Calloway, the protagonist of *The Good Old Boys*, into the conversation. Other classic titles worthy of argument include *The Day the Cowboys Quit, The Wolf and the Buffalo, Stand Proud*, and *The Man Who Rode Midnight* (all from TCU). Pick one and you'll not be disappointed.

For additional information about Kelton's career, his autobiography, *Sandhills Boy: The Winding Trail of a Texas Writer* (Forge Books), is recommended.

#  Lonesome Dove

## Larry McMurtry

Simon and Schuster, 1985; Pocket Books, 1988

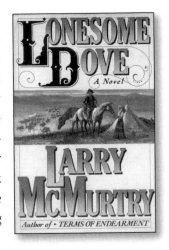

For all his public pleadings that today's Texas writers cling too stubbornly to tales of the Old West when their necessary attention should focus more on modern and urban stories, Larry McMurtry's greatest success is a product of the tried and true recipe. His *Lonesome Dove*—a frontier days western—not only won the Pulitzer Prize for Literature in 1986 but is today the book by which all other Texas fiction is measured. The reading world is made better for McMurtry having ignored his own dire warnings.

The heartwarming story of two faded Texas Rangers, August McCrae and Woodrow Call, who make one last cattle drive polishes the literary epic to a new brightness. There is high drama, a love story, and a moving portrait of man's attempt to achieve a final mark in life. Filled with fascinating characters and loosely based on numerous historic events, the book is a remarkable reading experience and was made into a television mini-series that broke viewing records and won seven Emmy Awards.

Rightfully judged the dean of Texas writers, McMurtry's body of work includes a number of other well-received novels—*Horseman, Pass By; Leaving Cheyenne; Terms of Endearment;* and *The Last Picture Show* among them. *In a Narrow Grave: Essays on Texas,* first published in 1968, is a valued book that continues to generate spirited discussion. For a look at McMurtry's career, Clay Reynolds' *Taking Stock: A Larry McMurtry Casebook* (SMU Press, 1989) is a worthwhile read.

 Texas

## James A. Michener

*Random House, 1985*

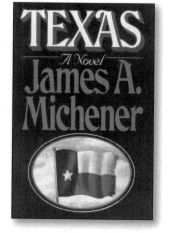

It is unlikely that any Texas-related book, before or since, has been viewed as the "event" that James Michener's bestselling novel became. From the time it was announced that the famed Pulitzer Prize winner was moving to the state to begin research until the 1,096-page book's publication, it kept tongues wagging on the cocktail circuit. This, everyone knew, was going to be a *big* book. Big-name author, even bigger subject.

After exhaustive research, Michener produced a fact-meets-fiction version of the state's history, beginning with the 1500s exploration by Spaniards Cabeza de Vaca and Francisco Vasquez de Coronado and traveling four and a half centuries to modern day. Along the way, Michener doesn't miss an important moment in the state's history, from the battle of the Alamo to the swearing in of presidents and the emergence of wildcatting oil billionaires and even its sports heroes. For good measure he tosses in an Indian raid here and there, details the cowboys' life, cotton farming and cattle ranching, and the political chicanery for which the state has been long infamous. As some reviewers have said of Michener's work, ask him the time and he'll tell you how the watch was built. That's certainly what he gave the readers of *Texas.*

So, was what resulted from all the hoopla and caused such a rush to the bookstores a great piece of historical fiction? Many critics said no. But it was—and remains—one of those books no literary Texan's bookshelf is complete without.

# The Gates of the Alamo

## Stephen Harrigan

Knopf, 2000, Penguin, 2001

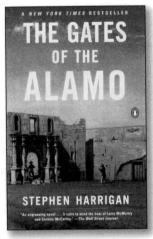

The literary land mine through which authors of historical fiction must navigate is no easy route. The trick is to revisit history in a manner than offers the reader a fascinating narrative woven into all the textbook background. Author Stephen Harrigan's acclaimed chronicle of the battle of the Alamo is a prime example of how it's properly done.

Telling his story through the innocent views of fictional characters—a devoted naturalist named Edmond McGowan, whose life's work is threatened by the oncoming war with Mexico; widowed innkeeper Mary Mott and her teenage son; and two members of General Santa Anna's forces—the oft-told tale takes on a new depth and personality. All the famous participants—Travis, Crockett, Bowie, et al—are keenly profiled in the 577 pages of Harrigan's classic; but it is the fictional vantage points of those he's added to the factual mix that elevates the book into rare air. The author's exhaustive research mixes perfectly with his remarkable writing talent.

The result is Texas history at its entertaining best.

And Harrigan hasn't stopped there. His most recent novel, the award-winning *Remember Ben Clayton*, is a poignant look at a Texas rancher's mission to honor his fallen son. In Harrigan's hands, Texas readers are well served.

# ⭐ The Son

## Philipp Meyer

Harper Collins, 2013

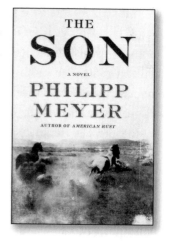

The landscape of Texas literature is littered with family sagas, some good, some less so. Few such books in memory, however, span almost 200 years and six generations and include a family tree which the reader will often find need to refer to.

Philipp Meyer's hefty and far-reaching novel stretches from the days of brutal Comanche raids to Texas' oil boom celebrations, offering the reader a ride along on a journey that is adventurous and joyous, tragic and heartbreaking. It has its fascinatingly irascible character, Eli McCullough, the first male child born in the Republic of Texas, abducted and raised by Indians and ultimately the mastermind of his family's rise to power and riches. There's soft-hearted son Peter, who bears the scars of the family's relentless greed. And Jeannie, Eli's hardened great-granddaughter who battles fiercely to make her mark in a modern man's world.

Meyer uses a variety of engaging techniques in his storytelling, from diary excerpts to recordings done by the WPA to the thoughts of an elderly bed-ridden woman whose body has worn out but whose recollections remain sharp. His research is that of a talented chronicler of Texas history and his writing is lyrical.

*The Son* is a story of dynasty building at any cost, love and betrayal, brutality and gentle reflection, and, ultimately, one of rise and fall. Which is to say it is a defining moment in the literature of the family saga.

# North to Yesterday

## Robert Flynn

Alfred A. Knopf, 1967; TCU Press, 1986

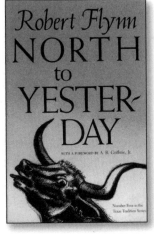

Since Andy Adams' *The Log of a Cowboy* was published in 1903, the cattle drive has been a familiar literary well to which Texas fiction writers have been drawn. There's Benjamin Capps' applauded *The Trail to Ogallala* and Larry McMurtry's epic *Lonesome Dove*. None of the above, however, will cause the reader to laugh aloud at the trials and tribulations encountered along the way.

Two decades before *Lonesome Dove*, Robert Flynn's award-winning *North to Yesterday* told much the same Old West story—but with a comic twist. The protagonist, Lampassas, is getting up in years with precious little time left to live out his dream of herding 2,000 range cattle to market. Never mind that the market hasn't existed for fifteen years or that he's woefully underfunded and seriously lacking in experience. He and his screwball crew even lose their horses along the way and wind up walking a too skinny, worthless herd to trail's end—where no buyers await.

The characters involved in this finely crafted misadventure are delightful, from Preacher, who signs on as cook because God commanded him to, to one of the wranglers who only wants to get to Kansas so he can marry a prostitute he'd met there years earlier.

Mixed into the wit and whimsy is a masterful and serious novel that just might well be more authentic in its recreation of time and place than the reader first imagines.

# The Trail to Ogallala

## Benjamin Capps

E. P. Dutton, 1964; TCU Press, 1985

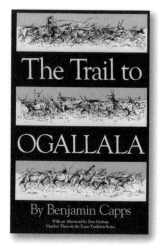

Over the years no Old West theme has been more fascinating to Texas novelists than the chronicling of the cattle drive. From Andy Adams to Elmer Kelton to Larry McMurtry, authors have found the dangers and high drama of men moving cattle northward a fertile platform for their storytelling. And few have done it better than Benjamin Capps in *The Trail to Ogallala*.

Winner of the Western Writers of America's Spur Award as 1964's Best Novel, it is far more than a vivid and well-researched account of men moving 3,000 head of cattle from south Texas toward Nebraska. Leaping well beyond the western formula, Capps populates his book with a fascinating cast of characters like young cowhand Billy Scott and a less than qualified trail boss named Blackie. Along the way their constant conflict is compounded by all the hazards a trail drive promises—renegade Indians, flooded rivers, death, and disappointment. And as he weaves his story, one of the most fascinating aspects the reader encounters is the unyielding terrain. The Plains themselves become a mesmerizing character.

You might argue which of Capps' impressive list of novels is, in fact, his best. Some would suggest *A Woman of the People*, the tale of two young white women captured by Comanches, and *The White Man's Road*, which views the faults and failure of the Indian Wars during settlement of the West. Or, if it's non-fiction you prefer, there's his brilliantly done *The Warren Wagontrain Raid*.

# The Train to Estelline

## Jane Roberts Wood

Temple Publishing, 1987; Random House, 1988;
University of North Texas Press, 2000

Seventeen-year-old Lucinda Richards leaves Bonham, Texas, in 1911 to accept a teaching position at a one-room schoolhouse on an isolated ranch in West Texas. In diary entries and letters to relatives, friends, and school officials, she tells of her experiences, her joys, fears, triumphs, and heartbreaks in a year and a half teaching children from grades one through ten—and of being courted and falling in love.

*The Train to Estelline* is the first novel in the Lucy Richards trilogy—the others being *A Place Called Sweet Shrub* (set in 1915) and *Dance a Little Longer* (set in 1931). *The Train to Estelline* was first published in 1987, and the trilogy was reissued in 2000. *Estelline* continues to appeal to women of various ages—younger women because the characters in the novels are young, and older women because the stories are set in a much earlier era.

A. C. Greene included *The Train to Estelline* in *The 50+ Best Books on Texas* in 1998, and it ranks as one of the all-time best-sellers for University of North Texas Press.

# Home from the Hill

## William Humphrey

Alfred A. Knopf, 1958; LSU Press, 1996

When the memorable story of the dysfunctional Hunnicutt family first appeared, some proclaimed that the Great Texas Novel had finally been written.

Set in the community of Clarksville during the 1930s, it is the story of family patriarch Captain Wade Hunnicutt, a demanding, hard-living cotton baron who is the region's richest resident. Then, there's his fragile wife Hannah, who likes absolutely nothing about the man she married. Caught in the middle is the novel's most finely drawn character, grown son Theron, who tries with little success to please both. It is a lusty story of a cursed family, haunted by money, murder, madness, and great irony.

Humphrey, a native of the region about which he writes, not only develops fascinating characters, large and small, but is without peer when describing the landscape in which his story is set. Few novelists can paint a scene more beautifully.

A successful film version starred Robert Mitchum as Wade Hunnicutt, Eleanor Parker as his wife, and George Hamilton as Theron. Humphrey was among the writers of the screenplay.

And it is not his only acclaimed work set in little Clarksville. *The Ordways* (1965) is the saga of four generations as the family moves from Tennessee to the Texas frontier after the Civil War. Which is the better book, *Home from the Hill* or *The Ordways?* Flip a coin, then enjoy both.

# ★ All the Pretty Horses

## Cormac McCarthy

Alfred A. Knopf, 1992; Vintage, 1993

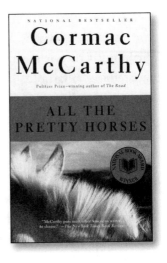

*All the Pretty Horses* received the National Book Award for Fiction in 1992, which seems adequate justification for selecting it as McCarthy's signature novel. However, it should be offered up as only a sampler of the author's highly acclaimed body of work. *Horses* was the first of what is now promoted as his Border Trilogy, followed by *The Crossing* and *Cities of the Plain*. Serious McCarthy devotees might argue that *Blood Meridian*, *The Road*, or *No Country for Old Men* are even better novels, but he remains best known for *All the Pretty Horses*.

Favored by literary intellectuals who teach college courses and write academic essays dissecting his work, as well as the general public looking only for a thoughtful, well-written read, *All the Pretty Horses* is a unique mixture of old-fashioned western with an ample dose of Gothic-like William Faulkner mixed in for good measure. At its core it is a provocative and thoughtful coming-of-age adventure.

*Horses* tells of sixteen-year-old John Grady Cole's dealing with the fact he is the last of several generations of Texas ranchers, denied the opportunity to do the only thing he's ever aspired to do. Accompanied by a friend, he makes a horseback trip into Mexico, meets another youngster who becomes a fellow traveler, falls in love, and gets an eye-opening view of a violent and unforgiving world he didn't know existed.

McCarthy's style is different—don't look for bothersome things like quotation marks—but his descriptions and storytelling are superb.

#  Hold Autumn in Your Hand

## George Sessions Perry

McGraw Hill, 1941; University of New Mexico Press, 1975

One of the early Texas novels that set the bar high for all writers to come, George Session Perry's masterpiece of farm life during the Depression received the National Book Award in 1942. The moving and eloquently written story takes the reader on a year-long journey with a Texas tenant farmer and his family as they battle hardships of the land and the times.

Sam Tucker is determined to prove that he can succeed as a bottomland farmer and persuades the owner to give him a year to produce a cotton crop. He, his wife, two young children, and Sam's elderly grandmother take up residence in a two-room shack. In a moving and well-paced style, Perry chronicles the day-to-day hardships, the intrusion of a mean-spirited neighbor, and, finally, the rages of Mother Nature that threaten defeat but, instead, only provide Tucker with renewed resolve.

In the years after its publication, *Hold Autumn in Your Hands* was favorably compared to John Steinbeck's classic *Grapes of Wrath* for its pitch-perfect portrait of Depression days and the families so drastically affected by them. *The New Yorker*, in fact, called it "a miniature *Grapes of Wrath* seen through optimistic glasses." It is Sam Tucker's strength and optimism that makes the book so memorable.

The book was made into a successful movie titled "The Southerner."

# ★ The Bottoms

## Joe R. Lansdale

Mysterious Press, 2000; Vintage Crime/Black Lizard, 2010

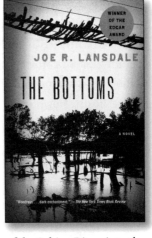

Mix a little William Faulkner with Harper Lee, then stir in a good amount of East Texas during the Depression and you've got a pretty good recipe for Joe Lansdale's award-winning novel that is part thriller, part coming-of-age story, and very much a memorable reading experience. *The Bottoms*, selected the best novel of the year by the Mystery Writers of America, vaulted cult hero Lansdale into the mainstream of American literature.

Set in 1933, a horrifying discovery by eleven-year-old Harry Crane and his sister launches a murder mystery that takes the reader along the banks of the Sabine River, into the hearts and minds of its struggling people, and visits the kind of legend that has given every child nightmares at one time or another. The story is told by Crane, who has turned eighty and finds it time to reflect back on the life-changing event.

With this lyrical novel, Lansdale combines all the storytelling excellence that has been the trademark of his prolific career, from his well-received Hap and Leonard mystery series to chilling horror stories that have won him numerous Bram Stoker Awards. Called by some reviewers a Texas version of *To Kill a Mockingbird*, *The Bottoms* is destined to be read by generations to come.

# ⭐ Rainwater

## Sandra Brown

Simon & Schuster, 2009

With more than sixty mega-seller romance and suspense novels and sales of eighty million and counting, Sandra Brown is certainly one of the best-selling Texas authors of all time, maybe even at the top of the list. However, in *Rainwater* she departed from the thriller genre to tell a tender story set in the Depression and inspired by a true family encounter.

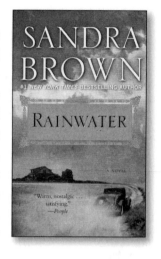

A dying man comes to spend his final days at a boarding house run by a mother, Ella, who also tends to her autistic and misunderstood young son, Solly. Solly has never uttered a word and the doctor advises her to put him in an institution.

The stranger, Mr. Rainwater, proves to be an extraordinary man who chooses to live out his dying days making a positive impact on the people with whom he comes into contact. He is able to get through to Solly in a way no one ever could, and he and Ella begin to fall in love.

Meanwhile, people are starving during the Depression, and a government program to slaughter cows and use them to feed hungry people is not working the way it should in their little Texas town. Mr. Rainwater confronts the inequities of the system. Readers have compared *Rainwater* to the Depression-era classic, *The Grapes of Wrath*.

Besides Brown, other popular and prolific contemporary female Texas novelists who set most of their stories in Texas include Jodi Thomas, Pamela Morsi, Susan Wittig Albert, Sarah Bird, Lori Wilde, Lisa Wingate, and Diane Kelly.

#  Roses

## Leila Meacham

Grand Central, 2010

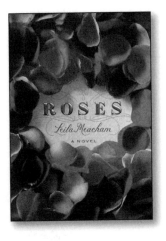

The 600-page saga traces the lives of three founding families of an East Texas town through three generations, focusing primarily on the lifelong relationships involving Mary Toliver, Percy Warwick, and Ollie DuMont. The story is told from three points of views—Mary's, Percy's, and Mary's great niece Rachel Toliver.

As the novel begins, Mary has rewritten her will, making major revisions that leave her long-time attorney puzzled and apprehensive. She won't explain her sudden change of heart, only hinting that they have to do with the "Toliver curse." It is 1985, and Mary does not want her beloved great niece to "sell her soul" for the sake of the family's cotton plantation.

So what is this curse and how has it affected three generations of three families? Mary flashes back to when it began to impact her life, in June 1916 when she inherited the plantation at age sixteen.

Despite its length, *Roses* is a fast, engrossing read, drawing comparisons to the classic epic *Gone with the Wind*. Meacham finished the novel at age seventy and it soared to the best-seller list and led to a prequel, *Somerset*, published in 2014.

To get the full story of the Tolivers, Warwicks, and DuMonts, start with *Somerset*, covering the period 1835 to 1900 when the families settled in Texas and started building their empires, with the "Toliver curse" haunting them from the beginning. In *Somerset* and *Roses*, Texas history comes alive in the triumphs and tragedies of six generations of the three interrelated families.

# ⭐ A Woman of Independent Means

## Elizabeth Forsythe Hailey

Viking Press, 1978; Penguin Books, 1998

The fictional autobiography of Bess Steed Garner, a social-climbing woman of mixed virtues, has earned legendary status not only for the fascinating journey it takes the reader on but for the manner in which it is chronicled.

Written as a series of letters which begin when Garner is a fourth grader at the turn of the century and taking her through an adulthood which is a mixture of triumph and tragedy, it is a coming-of-age novel, on one hand, and a keen look at the advancing role of women in society, on another.

As the reader follows Bess's growth over a sixty-nine year period, her letters become more thoughtful, more articulate, filled not only with personal observations and ambitions but unvarnished thoughts on everything from child-rearing and the disappointment she feels in the husbands she's chosen to philosophy and politics.

She is a complex woman who is driven, snobbish, and vain, yet witty, caring, and filled with strength and resolve. What author Hailey achieves with her protagonist's letters is a remarkable insight into one woman's travels from childhood to old age, all the while offering a fascinating view of the changing world in which she lives.

Considered one of the lasting classics of Texas letters, the book became a successful one-woman stage production, then an Emmy-nominated television mini-series.

# ⭐ Semi-Tough

## Dan Jenkins

Atheneum, 1972; DaCapo Press, 2006

When first published, with all its ribald humor, peerless parody, and zany cast of characters, Dan Jenkins' novel about life in the professional football fast lane set off a firestorm. It was irreverent, politically incorrect, and way beyond semi-funny. Think Dave Barry on steroids.

Featuring a cast of outrageous characters—running back Billy Clyde Puckett, wide receiver Shake Tiller, team owner Big Ed Bookman and his lovely daughter Barbara Jane—the story follows them during preparations for the Super Bowl. Along the way we meet self-improvement guru Friedrich Bismark who stirs the pot to a laugh-out-loud boil.

For all its charming one-liners, snappy dialogue, and outrageous situations, the book offers a dead-on look at life in the professional sports arena in the '70s. It's no wonder that it has been cited as one of the best sports books ever written, was made into a successful movie starring Burt Reynolds, and has become the yardstick against which other humorous fiction is measured.

A former Texas newspaperman who went on to become a celebrated staff member at *Sports Illustrated*, Jenkins' story-telling talents show brightly whether writing fiction or non-fiction. While *Semi-Tough* is generally considered his crowning achievement, his literary resume has plenty more to offer—like *Dead Solid Perfect*, *Baja Oklahoma*, and *Fast Copy*, to mention a few.

# ⭐ The Gay Place

## Billy Lee Brammer

Houghton-Mifflin, 1961; University of Texas Press, 1995

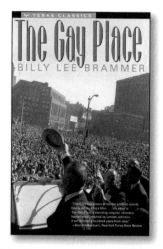

Bill Brammer's first and only novel was met with rave reviews and the disdain of a future president when it was published in 1961. Willie Morris judged it "the best novel about American politics in our time." Fellow writers like Gore Vidal and David Halberstam labeled it an instant classic.

Lyndon Johnson, after whom one of the lead characters—crude and ruthless governor Arthur Fenstemaker—was believed to have been modeled, responded less charitably. He saw to it that Brammer, who had once served as his press aide when he was Senate majority leader, was denied White House press credentials.

Actually three linked novellas—*The Flea Circus, Room Enough to Caper,* and *Country Pleasures*—the setting of Brammer's story is an unnamed state capital (clearly Austin) and offers up a bold and brassy view of life in the political fast lane in the '50s. His portrait of Austin is as fascinating as that of his ribald cast of characters.

Now, a half century later, *The Gay Place* continues to enjoy a cult following and has been reprinted numerous times. In 1963, plans were well underway for a movie version starring Paul Newman and Jackie Gleason, but the project was cancelled when President Kennedy was assassinated in Dallas.

Part of the continued fascination with the novel is the tragic aftermath suffered by Brammer. Though he made several false starts, he never completed another book. At the time of his death in 1978 he lived in Austin, working at odd jobs.

# Brownsville Stories

## Oscar Casares

Little, Brown and Company, 2003

Hidden away on the far tip of South Texas, the city of Brownsville had for years spent its bordertown life without a literary voice. Then came a gifted young fiction writer named Oscar Casares, introducing it and its fascinating people to the reading public.

With warmth, humor, and a style that causes one to wonder if the writer might be a distant relative of Mark Twain, his collection of stories gives life along the Rio Grande depth, meaning, and a rightful place in the state's literature.

The enchantment of *Brownsville Stories* is found in its neighborhoods, its Tex-Mex culture, and the innocent voices of those about whom he writes. From eleven-year-old Diego, who works in a fireworks stand, to Lola, in search of her stolen bowling ball, the stories have a quiet honesty that is touching and warm and reveals a great deal about the business of day-to-day living.

Casares deals with dreams and disappointments, realization and regret with a master's touch—funny at times, pensive at others. And he writes in a manner that suggests he's just eavesdropping on the community's life, able to make a neighbor's failure to return a prized hammer borrowed four years earlier into a life-changing experience.

These nine thoughtful tales of a place and its people provide a gentle reminder that they are, in their own way, unique and important to get to know.

# ⭐ The Vigil

## Clay Reynolds

St. Martin's Press, 1986; Texas Tech University Press, 2001

In the tiny Texas town of Agatite, it was unlikely that anything of lasting note would ever take place—until Imogene McBride's car broke down as she and precocious daughter Cora were in flight from a life of family misery back in Georgia. While they wait to continue their journey, seated together on a courthouse square bench, Cora decides to walk across the street to purchase an ice cream at the local drugstore. And disappears.

At that point, one might expect a traditional mystery novel to unfold. Instead, author Reynolds develops a moving story of devotion and desperation, of love lost and found played out by a memorable cast of characters. Imogene sits on the same bench for days, weeks, then months that turn into years, as she stoically awaits her daughter's return. The strange and tender vigil ultimately stretches through three decades.

To the townspeople, the determined mother becomes a local institution, affecting the lives of many in the community. Most moved is widowed local sheriff Ezra Holmes, who is drawn to the woman who sits endlessly, holding to a hope he himself has long since lost. Through their eyes, we get a keen and insightful view of life in a rural Texas town.

*The Vigil* is a beautifully written and engrossing portrait of people and the gentle pain and quiet desperation that guides their lives.

# ⭐ Bonney's Place

## Leon Hale

Shearer Publishing, 1981; Winedale Publishing, 2003

If the key elements to the success of a work of fiction are the creation of a memorable place and its people, newcomers to the craft would do themselves a favor by reading and learning from Leon Hale's charming portrait of beer joint culture in rural Texas.

A long-beloved Houston newspaper columnist with a keen ear for backwoods twangs and eye for the ordinary that blooms into the extraordinary, author Leon Hale's most lasting achievement is *Bonney's Place*. It is a pitch-perfect exploration of the consequences of backwoods suspicions, small sins, and miscarriages of justice, real and perceived.

There's the flawed but lovable Bonney McCamey, who sells a few groceries along with longnecks so his mother won't think he's actually running a roadhouse, and narrator Johnny Keller, who is dead certain that Bonney has swindled his Old Man, thus robbing him of his rightful inheritance. Joining in the fun and fussing are delightful characters like Turnip, Slat, Big Belly Ackers, and Rose-Mama. Think John Steinbeck's *Cannery Row* moved to the Piney Woods.

The visit to the fictional town of Farley and Bonney's beer joint is like sitting at the bar or shooting eight-ball with new friends who quickly tug at your heart and cause you to laugh aloud. And, before last call, you'll have learned a valuable life lesson or two.

Hale is the author of ten books, including another novel, *Addison*, several collections of his columns, and a memoir.

# Some Other Notable Titles

⭐ *The Bone Pickers* (Tech, 1958) is Al Dewlen's engaging family tale that follows the troubled Mungers as they rise from Dust Bowl poverty to become cattle and oil rich in the '50s. It is considered by many to be the best work of fiction set in the Texas Panhandle.

⭐ *The Color of Lightning* by Paulette Jiles (William Morrow, 2009) is a novel based on the true story of ex-slave Britt Johnson, who settled in Comanche territory in the 1860s. Johnson's family is attacked by Comanches while he is away on business. He vows to bring his family back together again, which is the principal plotline of this multi-faceted historical novel.

⭐ In *The Wonderful Country* (reprinted, TCU, 2002) artist/author Tom Lea offers a vivid portrait of life on the Texas-Mexico border in the 1870s. Featuring a troubled protagonist torn between two cultures, the enduring novel was filmed as a movie in 1958, starring Robert Mitchum.

⭐ *A Texas Jubilee*, James Ward Lee's delightful collection of short stories (TCU, 2012), is set in the fictional East Texas town of Bodark Springs, where people are struggling through the Great Depression with chins up and out, honky-tonking, sneaking around, fist-fighting, and being saved multiple times.

⭐ Two novels based in Dallas both deal with the assassination of President Kennedy. Edwin (Bud) Shrake's *Strange Peaches* (reprinted, John M. Hardy Publishing, 2007) is a mixture of bizarre comedy and tragedy and many of the lead characters are recognizable, even if their names are changed. Bryan Woolley's *November 22* (reprinted, Brown Books, 2013), detailing the twenty-four hours surrounding the event, also offers a rich and finely-written look at the city and its attitudes.

⭐ One of Texas' most endearing novelists, Shelby Hearon is at her best with *Hug Dancing* (reprinted, TCU, 2006). From the moment Cile Tate steps to the pulpit of her husband's Presbyterian church to boldly announce that she's leaving him and her children to return to a more comforting lifestyle, the reader is hooked. Hearon writes with warmth and a delightful helping of humor.

★ The most celebrated Texas author in recent years is Ben Fountain, whose *Billy Lynn's Long Halftime Walk* (Ecco, 2012) won the National Book Critics Circle Award and was a finalist for the National Book Award. The setting is a Dallas Cowboys game on Thanksgiving Day where members of Bravo Squad are being honored for their heroic service. Poignant and funny, it is satire at its best.

★ Few Texas authors have attracted the attention of literary scholars like novelist, poet, and professor Rolando Hinojosa-Smith, honored with the Lifetime Achievement Award from the National Book Critics Circle in 2014. His award-winning *Klail City Death Trip Series* (Arte Publico, 1973–2006), which has now grown to fifteen volumes, is set in a fictional Rio Grande Valley county, offering unique perspective into the Chicano culture. Hinojosa often writes in Spanish, then translates his works into English.

★ In 1925, *The Wind* (UT Press), a harrowing tale of a teenage orphan from Virginia who arrives in drought-plagued West Texas and is driven insane by the harsh new world she's entered, was published anonymously. Only later was it learned that the author of the highly acclaimed—and oft-criticized—novel was Baylor educator Dorothy Scarborough. Many scholars still consider it one of the best Texas novels ever written.

# PEOPLE

Everyone has a story, and you could fill a whole bookcase with biographies and autobiographies of interesting, influential, and innovative Texans and still not begin to cover them all.

What we've tried to do in this section is suggest a few titles that touch on some of the better known Texas personalities, and a few lesser known ones as well, from history, ranching, oil, politics, medicine, music, and literature. Sports and crime figures are covered in other sections.

# ⭐ Sam Houston

## James L. Haley

University of Oklahoma Press, 2004

At last count, no fewer than sixty biographies of the legendary figure who helped guide Texas into statehood have been published. Which is to say the colorful career of Sam Houston, soldier and statesman, has been a lasting source of fascination to historians as well as those who delight in learning how Texas battled to become part of the Union.

From a crowded bookshelf, two of the bios have risen to the top. First, there was Marquis James' *The Raven: A Biography of Sam Houston* which earned the Pulitzer Prize in 1930 (reprinted by University of Texas Press, 1988). For decades it stood alone as the definitive Houston bio. Then came Haley's remarkable entry after fifteen years of research. From scholars to casual readers, his now wins the honor of being judged the best, if only by a nose.

In a pleasing non-academic style, Haley traces the enigmatic leader through a career as governor of Tennessee to respected military leader, president of the Republic of Texas, U.S. Senator, and governor of Texas. And while he fashions a valuable and engaging history of the state where Houston's legend flourished, the author also provides the reader with a more intimate look at the person, from his life lived among the Cherokees and his kinship with Andrew Jackson to the mystery of a first marriage that lasted only eleven weeks.

The Houston about whom Haley writes was as complex as he was brilliant. So were the times in which he lived. As Texas historian Elliott West noted upon publication of *Sam Houston*, "all future scholarship on Houston and Texas will have to reckon with this striking and substantial book."

# The Trail Drivers of Texas

### Edited by J. Marvin Hunter

First published 1924–1925; UT Press edition, 1985, 1993

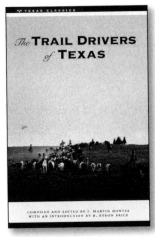

This 1,100 page anthology has been called "the bible" of the old-time cattle drives and "one of the finest works ever produced on the cattle industry." The book's lengthy subtitle pretty much summarizes the contents: "Interesting Sketches of Early Cowboys and Their Experiences on the Range and on the Trail during the Days That Tried Men's Souls—True Narratives Related by Real Cowpunchers and Men Who Fathered the Cattle Industry in Texas."

The hefty volume includes about 300 mostly first-person accounts by the men (and some women) of the old cattle drives and to some extent their lives after their cattle-driving days were over.

Two related books are *Black Cowboys of Texas* and *Texas Women on the Cattle Trails* (Texas A&M, 2000 and 2006), both edited by Sara R. Massey. African American cowboys had to overcome discrimination and prejudice, relying on their toughness, courage, and competence to gain the respect of other cowboys and their bosses. The volume on women includes sixteen biographical essays of women who accompanied Texas cattle drives between 1868 and 1889.

J. Evetts Haley's biography of *Charles Goodnight: Cowman and Plainsman*, published in 1936 and still in print from the University of Oklahoma Press, is probably the best known and most highly regarded single biography concerning the cattle drive days and early ranching history in Texas.

Also, C. L. Douglas's classic *Cattle Kings of Texas* (reprinted by State House, 1989) is a very readable and authoritative account of legendary Texas ranching pioneers.

 # Interwoven
*A Pioneer Chronicle*

## Sallie Reynolds Matthews

Originally published 1936;
Texas A&M University Press, 1982

INTERWOVEN
*A Pioneer Chronicle*

By Sallie Reynolds Matthews
*Drawings by E. M. Schiwetz*
MEMORIAL PRINTING

*Interwoven* is on nearly every major list of top Texas books, including A. C. Greene's *50+ Best Books on Texas* and John H. Jenkins' *Basic Texas Books.* Jenkins called it the "best book on Texas ranch life from a woman's perspective."

The book, intended for family and friends when it was first published in 1936, covers the first thirty-eight years of the writer's life, from 1861 to 1899, and focuses on the Reynolds and Matthews families whose lives became "interwoven" through marriages and mutual ranching enterprises.

Sallie Reynolds married John "Bud" Matthews when she was just fifteen in 1876 and they would have nine children, seven of whom survived to adulthood. The youngest child, Watkins Reynolds "Watt" Matthews, would live to be ninety-eight and become a ranching legend in his own right though the family's Lambshead Ranch outside Albany.

Sallie Reynolds Matthews proved in her memoirs to be a reliable historian and excellent story-teller as she related tales about Indian raids, family life on the frontier, life at old Fort Davis and then Fort Griffin, early-day ranching in the area, and the establishment of Albany. Her recollections formed the basis for much of the history and lore reflected in the "Fort Griffin Fandangle" outdoor musical performances staged every year in Albany.

In addition to *Interwoven,* Texas A&M has published three related books— *Lambshead Before Interwoven: A Texas Range Chronicle 1848–1878* by Frances Mayhugh Holden; *Lambshead Legacy: The Ranch Diary of Watt R. Matthews,* edited by Janet M. Neugebauer, and focusing on Watt's daily life from 1951 to 1980; and *Watt Matthews of Lambshead,* photographs and text by Laura Wilson, published in 1989 and updated in 2007 to reflect his death.

# ⭐ I'll Gather My Geese

## Hallie Crawford Stillwell

Texas A&M University Press, 1991

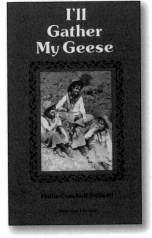

"When writing this book," Hallie Stillwell begins, "I did not aspire to write a masterpiece. I wanted only to leave with my children and grand-children something about my life on the raw frontier of Texas. My small role in 'taming the West' was different from that of other women who lived there because of the many years I spent in the saddle playing an active part in the cattle business."

In 1918, at age twenty, she married Roy Stillwell, who owned a hardscrabble ranch outside of Marathon near the Mexico border. She immediately plunged into working the ranch from horseback while sharing a bedroll with Roy on the floor of their twelve by sixteen "ranch house." She overheard ranch hands muttering, "That woman schoolteacher won't last six months down here in this Godforsaken country."

They were wrong. She not only lasted, she made the ranch a home where she would raise two sons and a daughter and keep the ranch afloat through epidemics, droughts, war, and her husband's illness.

The title of the book comes from an admonition from Hallie's father in 1916 when she set off to be a teacher on the Rio Grande border. He told her she was going on a wild goose chase, and she responded, "Then I'll gather my geese."

She was ninety-three when the book was published. A sequel, *My Goose Is Cooked*, published after she died at age ninety-nine in 1997, includes the last ten chapters of her memoir, picking up after her husband died in 1948.

# The Big Rich

*The Rise and Fall of the Greatest Oil Fortunes*

## Bryan Burrough

Penguin, 2009

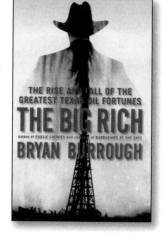

Bryan Burrough tells the story of Texas oil from the standpoint of four independent Texas wildcatters who struck it rich and made a name for themselves on the national stage. *The Big Rich* focuses on the oilmen who became known as the Big Four—Roy Cullen of Houston, Sid Richardson of Fort Worth, and Clint Murchison and H. L. Hunt of Dallas.

Burrough dug deeply into family and petroleum lore to present a fascinating and detailed account of how oil fortunes were made, flaunted, and sometimes lost from the 1920s through the 1980s and into the new century.

At one time or another, most of these men were hailed by one publication or another as "the richest man in the world." They were not shy in flashing their money around, whether through private island resorts, ultraconservative political causes, or lavish homes, parties, hotels, and ranches that attracted top-name celebrities. They were featured on the covers of national magazines and became something of an icon—the ultra-rich Texas oilman. Books were written about them, movies and TV shows made about them.

The second generation inherited the hundreds of millions, even billions, but in most cases had to split it up among the heirs. Then the problems started, as heirs made their own decisions. In an epilogue, Burrough provides a concise wrap-up of what happened to the children of the Big Four.

# Profiles in Power
*Twentieth Century Texans in Washington*

## Edited by Kenneth E. Hendrickson Jr., Michael L. Collins, Patrick Cox

University of Texas Press, new edition, 2004

The collection profiles fourteen Texans who wielded considerable clout in Washington during the twentieth century, beginning with Edward M. House, who became President Woodrow Wilson's closest adviser.

Others include Morris Sheppard, author of the Prohibition amendment; Houston financier Jesse H. Jones, once called "the second most powerful man in Washington"; longtime senator Tom Connally, a key figure in creating the United Nations; House Speakers Sam Rayburn, a revered statesman, and Jim Wright; Senators John Tower, Ralph Yarborough, and Lloyd Bentsen; congressmen Henry B. Gonzalez and Barbara Jordan; Vice President John Nance Garner; and, of course, Presidents Lyndon Johnson and George H. W. Bush. (George W. Bush held office in the twenty-first century.)

The profiles, by fourteen contributing historians, are fifteen to twenty-five pages each and deal not only with their political careers but also include interesting personal anecdotes and details. For example, Vice President Garner got his nickname "Cactus Jack" as a young state representative in Austin because of his unsuccessful effort to get the cactus adopted as the state flower.

The editors admit that good cases could be made for other influential Texans in Washington, such as presidential confidantes James Baker and Robert Strauss, former senator Phil Gramm, former governor John Connally, longtime House Banking Committee chairman Wright Patman, and others.

Of those selected, the editors contend, "in each case, they made major and sometimes colossal contributions to the development of the United States."

# ☆ The Path to Power
*The Years of Lyndon Johnson, Part I*

## Robert Caro

Alfred A. Knoff, 1982

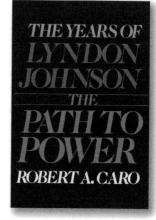

A New York-born, Ivy League-educated author is viewed as the undisputed expert on the life and times of President Lyndon Johnson. Two-time Pulitzer Prize winner Robert Caro has spent the lion's share of his professional life researching and writing about the powerful Texan, with four volumes published and a fifth in the works.

While each book offers revealing information and new perspectives, for the purposes of gaining a better understanding of Texas the first in the series is most highly recommended.

In *The Path to Power*, Caro examines in exhaustive detail the early life of the young man from Johnson City. The bestselling book took seven years to research and write (Caro even moved to Texas for an extended time to meet Johnson associates and view the landscape of his upbringing) and provides the reader insight into his Hill Country heritage and early political ambitions. The first book of the massive biography takes LBJ from boyhood to his failed campaign for the U.S. Senate in 1941, offering a fascinating look at Texas politics at the time.

For those who wish to follow Johnson's full career, read Caro's *Means of Ascent* (1990), *Master of the Senate* (2002) and *The Passage of Power* (2012).

For a more personal slant, try Lady Bird Johnson's *White House Diary* (Funk & Wagnalls, 1970) and *Ruffles and Flourishes* by Liz Carpenter (Texas A&M, 1993).

# Barbara Jordan
*Speaking the Truth with Eloquent Thunder*

## Edited by Max Sherman

University of Texas Press, 2007

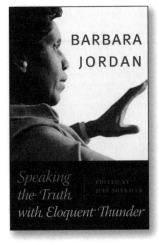

It is safe to say that probably no Texans—and few Americans—have been as eloquent in defending the Constitution and civil liberties as was Barbara Jordan (1936–1996). As a state senator, U.S. congresswoman, and political science professor, her magnificent voice was matched only by her resolute commitment to integrity and ethics in public service.

This small volume by Max Sherman, published more than a decade after Jordan's death, includes the text of nine of her speeches, accompanied by a DVD of Jordan delivering four of those speeches, including two keynote addresses to the Democratic National Convention and the address that gained her a national following—her prime-time televised remarks during the impeachment hearing of Richard Nixon: "My faith in the Constitution is whole, it is complete, it is total. And I am not going to sit here and be an idle spectator to the diminution, the subversion, the destruction of the Constitution."

With this book and DVD, readers in the twenty-first century can not only revisit Barbara Jordan's words on paper, they can experience her proclamations first hand.

For those wanting to read more about Jordan's life, check out Mary Beth Rogers' 380-page biography, *Barbara Jordan: American Hero* (Bantam, 1998).

#  Bob Bullock

*God Bless Texas*

## Dave McNeely and Jim Henderson

University of Texas Press, 2008

The trademark of modern-day Texas politics has been its turbulence, stirred by larger-than-life men and women elected to serve the needs of the people. None was bigger nor stirred more vigorously than Democratic power broker Bob Bullock who climbed from one office to another to become the state's lieutenant governor in the '90s.

At every stop—assistant attorney general, secretary of state, and state comptroller—he increased the influence of each office he held, and by the end of the twentieth century was generally recognized as the most powerful figure in Texas politics.

He was a man of myriad facets, devoted to the people, stubborn with a thundering temper, a political genius, and, for most of his life, a hard drinker. (How can you not want to read a biography that includes a chapter titled "Whiskey, Women, Airplanes and Guns"?)

Bullock, who worked in public service from 1956, when elected to the Texas House of Representatives, until his death in 1999, understood the inner workings of the political machine like none other. He was able to break down party barriers to get things done.

What authors Dave McNeely and Jim Henderson have accomplished is a well-researched and well-written biography, telling the story of one of the most colorful figures in Texas political history and providing an inside look into how the political wars are fought in Austin.

# 100,000 Hearts:
*A Surgeon's Memoir*

## Denton Cooley

University of Texas Press, 2011

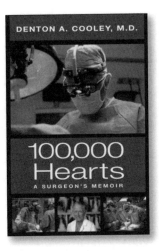

Dr. Denton Cooley, a pioneer and pivotal figure in the field of heart surgery, was once asked in a medical liability trial if he considered himself the best heart surgeon in the world.

"Yes," Cooley said he replied. The lawyer then asked if that wasn't being "rather immodest."

"Perhaps," Cooley responded. "But, remember, I'm under oath."

Cooley told his story in *100,000 Hearts: A Surgeon's Memoir* as he approached his ninetieth birthday. Chapters in Cooley's memoir included his growing up in Houston as a dentist's son, going to UT on a basketball scholarship, the early years and evolution of heart surgery, the development of the Total Artificial Heart, and his family life.

Cooley offered his take on the highly publicized rivalry and rift with his mentor, Dr. Michael DeBakey. They eventually reconciled in 2007, a few months before DeBakey died.

Cooley said he tried to foster "harmony and productiveness among my staff" while DeBakey "was stern and abusive toward his residents and staff" and "could be extremely vindictive."

"To be fair," Cooley added, "our ambitions and egos also got in each other's way. When two men with strong ambitions are put together, conflict is almost inevitable,"

In his memoirs, Cooley said, "I've tried to be respectful and considerate, to avoid gossip, and to omit surgical details that might ruin your lunch."

# ⭐ Willie Nelson
*An Epic Life*

## Joe Nick Patoski

Little Brown and Company, 2008

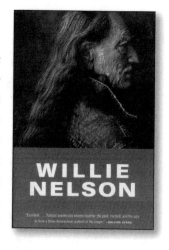

Texas can boast of being the home place of U.S. presidents, big money wheelers and dealers, and folk legends famous and infamous, but few have made more of an impact on the state's modern-day culture than country music icon Willie Nelson. From a hardscrabble beginning in the tiny community of Abbott to a traveling life entertaining in dirt road honkytonks and glitzy venues, Willie's following borders on a religious devotion.

And no writer has more closely followed the life and career of Nelson than author Joe Nick Patoski. Over an almost four decade journalism career, he had chronicled the rise to fame—from a frustrated door-to-door vacuum cleaner salesman to celebrated songwriter and singer—before taking on the task of this thorough and well-crafted biography. And when it was done he had produced a work that is a tale of true Texas grit and a state's devotion to beer-drinking, she-done-me-wrong music.

With exhaustive research and interviews with a Who's Who of the genre, *Willie Nelson* touches all the bases—from hard times to hero worship, life on the road, women, whiskey, and pot-smoking—and recounts the days when Austin magically emerged as a mecca for outlaw musicians.

More than an award-winning, in-depth biography of a folk hero, it is a valuable history of the kind of music that has long been the anthem of Texas.

For Nelson's own take on his life and career, *Willie: An Autobiography* (Cooper Square Press, 2000), written with Bud Shrake, is also an entertaining and insightful read, as is Willie's more recent *Roll Me Up and Smoke Me When I Die* (William Morrow, 2012).

# The Voice of an American Playwright

*Interviews with Horton Foote*

## Gerald C. Wood and Marion Castleberry

Mercer University Press, 2012

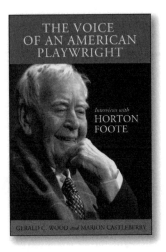

Horton Foote was a beloved and award-winning playwright, winner of two Academy Awards, an Emmy, and a Pulitzer Prize among many others. His upbringing in Wharton, Texas, formed the basis for much of his work. As he told an interviewer, "No matter how far away I've been—New York, London, Hollywood—half of me is always thinking about Wharton, trying to figure out some aspect of this life back here."

He was born in 1916 and died in 2009 and over the years sat patiently for numerous interviews with theater professionals, journalists, authors, academicians, and others. This collection of twenty-five interviews includes a chronology, a list of his published works, and a selected bibliography.

In the interviews, he discusses the writing process, the storytelling tradition, sense of place, family life, collaboration, political and religious views, themes like humanism, change, and courage, and many of his 100 plays, screenplays, and television productions. Most notable among those are *To Kill a Mockingbird*, *The Trip to Bountiful*, and *Tender Mercies*.

Actor Robert Duvall called Foote "the great American voice," and that gentle, soft-spoken yet candid voice comes alive in these interviews conducted from 1973 to shortly before his death in 2009.

# All the Best, George Bush
*My Life in Letters and Other Writings*

## George H. W. Bush

Scribner, 1999; revised edition, 2013

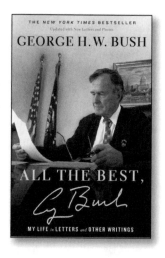

The Bushes—George and Barbara, and George W. and Laura—all produced best-selling memoirs of their years in public life, and other books have been written about them, before, during and after their presidencies. We have chosen to include this one by the elder George Bush because of the nature of the book—a comprehensive collection of letters, memos, and diary entries that reveal not only his policy and personal insights but also his sense of humor, his warmth, and his deep family relationships.

The book begins with letters written home during his service as a Navy pilot in World War II, followed by correspondence from his early years in Texas and his election to the U.S. House of Representative in 1966. Succeeding chapters include letters and reflections while serving as U.S. ambassador to the U.N., chairman of the Republican National Committee during the Watergate years, head of the U.S. liaison in China, director of the CIA, unsuccessful candidate for president in 1980, vice president for eight years, winning the presidency in 1988, his four years in the Oval Office, then losing his bid for re-election in 1992, and life after the White House to 1998. The revised edition updated the collection with a chapter of correspondence through 2012.

Included are letters written to his children and grandchildren at various stages of his life, letters to friends suffering personal crises, and such oddities as a note to the Hawaii Islands Cockroach Racing Association saluting his entry in the race, the Oval Officeroach, and his views on hamburgers expressed in a letter to *Texas Monthly.*

# Some Other Notable Titles

⋆ *Stephen F. Austin: Empresario of Texas* by Gregg Cantrell (Yale University Press, 2001) was the first major biography of Austin since Eugene Barker's in 1925. Cantrell's image of the "Father of Texas" was that of a more colorful, complex, and engaging man of action than previously portrayed.

⋆ *Texas Tears and Texas Sunshine: Voices of Frontier Women,* edited by Jo Ella Powell Exley, is a collection of first-person narratives by sixteen pioneer women about their lives on the harsh Texas frontier, from before the Texas Revolution through the Indian raids and cattle drives to the taming of the frontier. First published in 1986, it has become one of Texas A&M University Press's all-time best-sellers.

⋆ Bert Almon reviewed the autobiographies—and lives—of nineteen Texans in *This Stubborn Self* (TCU, 2002), with essays on Sallie Reynolds Matthews, Gertrude Beasley, Hallie Stillwell, A. C. Greene, Pat Mora, Charlie C. White, and others.

⋆ *Let Me Tell You What I've Learned: Texas Wisewomen Speak* by P. J. Pierce (UT, 2002) comprises interviews with two dozen influential Texas women about what advice and insights they would pass on to young people. Interviewees include prominent figures in politics, art, sports, education, journalism, medicine, and business.

⋆ No Texas journalist chronicled the state's zany political landscape with the bold and brash style of the late Molly Ivins. Her column appeared in hundreds of newspapers, and book collections of her writings (like *Molly Ivins Can't Say That, Can She?*) were bestsellers. *Molly Ivins: A Rebel Life* (Public Affairs, 2009) by Bill Minutaglio and W. Michael Smith offers a good way to get to know her.

⋆ Probably no one in the history of Texas A&M had more impact on the future of the university than World War II hero James Earl Rudder, who went on to be president of A&M at a critical period in the school's history. His story, focusing on his wartime and university service, is told in *Rudder: From Leader to Legend* by Thomas M. Hatfield (A&M, 2011).

★ As Jan Reid's biography, *Let the People In: The Life and Times of Ann Richards* (UT, 2012), clearly notes, few modern-day women have stood beneath a brighter spotlight than Richards. Reid details her remarkable rise to political power, from her keynote address at the 1988 Democratic National Convention to serving as governor of Texas.

★ Mary Karr's *The Liars' Club: A Memoir* (Penguin, 2005), a stark yet darkly humorous examination of growing up in a volatile East Texas family in the '60s, is considered one of the most powerful memoirs ever written by a Texas author.

★ From the dusty streets of Roby to the mean ones of Fort Worth and on to the bright lights of Las Vegas, Doyle Brunson's *The Godfather of Poker* (Cardoza Publishing, 2009), written with Mike Cochran, is a page-turning life story that reads like fiction. A two-time winner of the World Series of Poker, high stakes gambler Brunson once bet a million dollars on a single round of golf and has rubbed elbows with sportsmen almost as fascinating as he is.

★ A finalist for the National Book Award, Domingo Martinez's *The Boy Kings of Texas: A Memoir* (Lyons Press, 2012) is a highly-acclaimed witty and gritty first-person account of growing up in a barrio in border-town Brownsville.

★ She is called one of America's greatest storytellers, winning the Pulitzer Prize for her novel *Ship of Fools* and a National Book Award for her collection of short stories, yet Katherine Anne Porter, born in Indian Gap, Texas, rarely wrote about her home state. In Joan Givner's *Katherine Anne Porter: A Life* (University of Georgia Press, 1991), however, readers get a revealing look at Porter's early days as well as her remarkable career.

# PLACE

With more than 268,000 square miles, Texas offers a diversity of landscapes, from the beaches and forests in the south and east to the mountains and prairies of the north and west to the rugged beauty of the Hill Country and the sprawling growth of cities, all connected by ribbons of rivers and highways.

The books in this section reflect and salute that diversity, that sense of place, through gentle essays, spectacular photographs, and straightforward accounts of natural and man-made wonders and disasters.

# Adventures with a Texas Naturalist

## Roy Bedichek

University of Texas Press, 1947, 1975

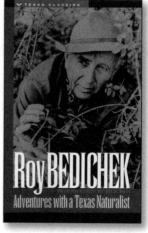

For a time the early day ranks of Texas authors who had earned national recognition was the property of two men—legends J. Frank Dobie and Walter Prescott Webb. Seeking to add another voice, they urged friend and educator Roy Bedichek to come aboard, helping raise funds so that he might take a year's leave from his teaching. Dobie even offered lodging at his ranch.

The result was the remarkable *Adventures with a Texas Naturalist,* an introspective and expansive book that first appeared in 1947. With its publication, Texas had what literary historians now look back on as the Big Three. And it is safe to say that today it is Bedichek's master work that continues to be the best read of any written by the triumvirate of gifted authors.

The essays ring true in the clear voice of a writer fascinated by all things around him—the flowers and fauna, birds and animals, and the land and the people who have inhabited it. Neither scientist nor philosopher, Bedichek comes across as both as he promotes a unique view that all things that leave their footprints are related, intertwined in a unique kinship that gives art and understanding to the world through which he traveled. While many writings six decades old have become irrelevant, this one remains evergreen.

The latest edition includes an introduction by modern-day naturalist Rick Bass.

#  Goodbye to a River

## John Graves

Alfred Knopf, 1961; Vintage, 2002

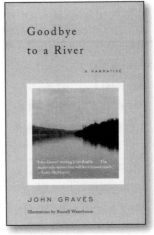

At first blush it might sound simplistic: in the '50s, a man takes a three-week canoe trip along a river, recording what he sees, recalling what was once there, all the while weaving his own wit and country boy philosophy into the narrative. That, however, would be akin to saying Henry David Thoreau's *Walden* is nothing more than a book about a man living alone in the wilderness.

John Graves' signature work is deemed by many to be the best book written by a Texas author.

Concerned that a series of proposed dams along the Brazos River would forever alter the landscape and cause an environmental change that promised nothing good, Graves set out on his voyage and first wrote of his findings for *Holiday* magazine. Such was the positive response that he returned to the typewriter, adding insightful history and folklore of the region, additional personal observations, and produced an award-winning book that still stands as one of the most lyrical and thoughtful examinations of Texas ever offered. Graves ponders the harmony of nature, the importance that the past plays on the present—and future—all the while offering well-researched Texas history.

Other Graves books well worth a read include *Hard Scrabble; From a Limestone Ledge; Blue & Some Other Dogs,* and *The Last Running.*

# ⭐ A Personal Country

## A. C. Greene

Knopf, 1969; University of North Texas Press, 1998

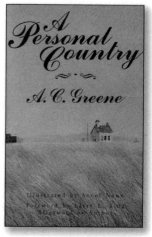

A moving and well-crafted visit to a man's home—and heartland—*A Personal Country* is the *tour de force* of author Greene's distinguished writing career.

It is an introspective and loving look at that sprawling region of the state known as West Texas and takes the reader along on a charming ride through its history, its people, its moods, and personality. From the days of Indian raids to oil booms, its religion and politics, and, most importantly, its unique breed of people, Greene writes of a sentimental journey through a sometimes harsh, always fascinating part of the state to construct a classic of Texas literature.

Through childhood recollections, portraits of colorful characters, remembered pleasures and life-changing occurrences, accounts of hard times and prosperity, what emerges is a large and loving picture of a landscape that is unique in ways both large and small. From the endless grasslands to the streets of its cities, the hardscrabble to oil-rich lifestyles, and the simple times recalled and comfort taken from a place that molded his personality, Greene makes West Texas an unforgettable character in this well-received and lasting achievement.

In his fiction (*The Highland Park Woman*) and history (Edgar Award finalist *The Santa Claus Bank Robbery*), Greene's focus was always on a memorable and tightly woven mixture of people and places.

# Great Lonely Places
# of the Texas Plains

**Poems by Walt McDonald**

**Photographs by Wyman Meinzer**

Texas Tech University Press, 2003

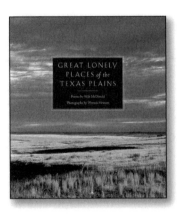

Bring together the eloquent ruminations of a Texas Poet Laureate and the striking color images of the Texas State Photographer, both native West Texans, and the stark beauty of West Texas comes alive in this graceful collection of seventy-seven pairs of poems and photographs.

McDonald and Meinzer explained the process as they sorted through thousands of poems and photographs to put the book together. "We kept only the photos and poems that together and on their own both startled and delighted, that shocked and jostled. Throughout the selection process came the delight of recognizing our common heritage in those lonely but great places of the Plains, those unexpected and too often unnoticed details that sometimes get lost between horizon and sky, those people we've loved and learned from."

The nine by eleven book is divided into six sections and includes such poems as "Ten Miles in Every Direction," "The Winter Daddy Died," "Nights on the Brazos," "Uncle Oscar and the Art of Carving," "The Art of Growing Old," and "Gardens of Sand and Cactus." Each verse is presented on one page, facing a page with the companion photograph, designed with plenty of white space to encourage readers to gently immerse themselves in the lyrics and the landscapes.

Wyman Meinzer's spectacular photographs of the Texas sky are showcased in two other books—*Texas Sky* and *Between Heaven and Texas* (both from UT Press)—and he teamed up with author John Graves to produce tributes to *Texas Rivers* and *Texas Hill Country* (also UT).

# The Big Thicket Guidebook
*Exploring the Backroads and History of Southeast Texas*

## Lorraine G. Bonney

University of North Texas Press, 2011

*The Big Thicket Guidebook* is an encyclopedic reference book, anthology, and travel guide to the ecological phenomenon and geographical region known for its forests, swamps, wild animals, colorful fauna, and even more colorful legends.

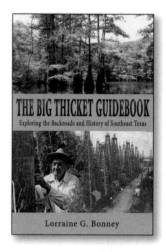

The first 200 of the book's 800-plus pages are devoted to a history of the Thicket and lively stories concerning nine Southeast Texas towns—Beaumont, Batson, Saratoga, Liberty, Sour Lake, Kountze, Silsbee, Woodville, and Jasper.

But the heart of the book is the almost 600 pages devoted to fifteen primary tours and twenty-four secondary tours of the Thicket, complete with maps, history, folklore, personalities, natural wonders, mile markers, and points of reference.

Readers will find in these pages accounts of bear hunting, oil booms, sawmills, timber barons, ghost towns, ghost stories, family feuds, murders, folk doctors, and maverick editors and congressmen.

It's more than most readers might ever want to know about the Big Thicket, but it is an incredible, valuable, and approachable resource, or as Professor Pete Gunter puts it in the introduction, "an unlikely compendium of local hearsay, careful archival research, wild improbable stories, and data dug out of courthouse records."

# Whooping Crane
*Images from the Wild*

## Photographs by Klaus Nigge

Texas A&M University Press, 2010

The Whooping Crane, once near extinction when the count was down to fifteen adult birds, has made a slow but steady comeback, with more than 300 now in habitats. The cranes winter in Texas and summer in Canada, and German photographer Klaus Nigge spent months photographing them in both locations. A hundred and fifty-six of his color photographs were collected into what is probably one of the most elegant books ever published in Texas.

Nigge recorded the daily activities of one family of cranes over several weeks at the Aransas National Wildlife Refuse on the Texas Gulf Coast, and also photographed the birth of a chick at the Wood Buffalo National Park in Alberta, Canada. The birds arrive in Texas in late October or early November and stay until March, when they fly to their Canadian breeding ground.

Visitors may view the cranes from the forty-foot observation tower at Aransas National Wildlife Refuge or from a boat tour out of Rockport. Readers of *Whooping Crane: Images from the Wild* get an even better view.

Krista Schlyer, a member of the International League of Conservation Photographers, introduces the book with an informative essay on the history of the whooping crane and the fight to preserve the species.

# Texas Mountains

## Photography by Laurence Parent
## Text by Joe Nick Patoski

University of Texas Press, 2001

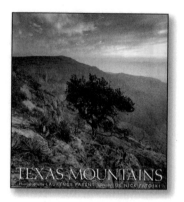

Texas mountains are grouped in the far western part of the state known as the Trans-Pecos, with about forty mountain ranges over eight sparsely populated counties, with the exception of El Paso. As mountains go, Texas' ranges hardly measure up to those in Colorado and New Mexico, but as Patoski and Parent note in their beautiful tribute to *Texas Mountains*, "they're breathtaking taken on their own terms."

"Since the Texas Mountains are so isolated from Texas' population centers and not easy to get to," writes Patoski, "not too many people know about them." But thanks to Parent's camera and Patoski's pen, readers are given a rare, full-color tour of the Texas peaks, the tallest of which is Guadalupe Peak at 8,749 feet. Much of the property is private and is otherwise inaccessible, making this collection of photographs not only the best way to see the mountains but perhaps the only way.

Parent and Patoski teamed up on two other photographic projects, both from UT Press—*Big Bend National Park* (2006) and *Texas Coast* (2005). Parent also has produced a gorgeous and very reasonably priced portfolio of varied Texas scenes and landscapes—from beaches and forests to deserts, canyons, and mountains—in his 112-page tribute, *Texas: Portrait of a State* (Graphic Arts Books, 2013).

# ⬠ Living Witness

*Historic Trees of Texas*

## Text and Photos by Ralph Yznaga

Texas A&M University Press, 2012

In words and color pictures, *Living Witness* tells the stories of thirty-seven spectacular and notable Texas trees, most of them oaks. Among the trees included are:

The Goose Island Oak in Goose Island State Park near Rockport. The tree is believed to be at least a thousand years old.

The Treaty Oak in Austin, once voted the most perfect specimen of an oak tree in the United States.

The Fleming Oak in Comanche, which Martin Fleming credited with saving his life from a Comanche attack. He huddled in the space between two large trunks.

The Century Tree in College Station, considered the most romantic spot on the Texas A&M campus and the site of countless proposals and weddings.

The Heart O' Texas Oak near Mercury, a modest tree that stands at the exact geographic center of the state.

The Kissing Oak at San Marcos, where Sam Houston kissed admiring women while campaigning for governor in 1857.

The Matrimonial Oak in San Saba, where at least three weddings took place on the same day in 1911—and many more before and since.

The Runaway Scrape Oak in Gonzales, where General Houston gathered his ragtag army in March 1836 and began retreating eastward until reaching San Jacinto.

Besides the book's historical importance, it also stands as a reminder to Texans to be vigilant in protecting these significant natural resources.

# ★Texas Disasters
*True Stories of Tragedy and Survival*

## Mike Cox

Globe Pequot Press, 2006

Mike Cox examines twenty of the state's worst calamities, chronicling those who perished—and survived—in hurricanes, tornadoes, and blizzards as well as diseases, fires, floods, explosions, and plane crashes in Texas. The book begins in 1554 with the lost Spanish fleet and continues through the devastating hurricanes of 2005.

Hurricanes wiped out the town of Indianola in 1875 and 1886 and changed Galveston forever in 1900. Fire devastated the downtown of Paris in 1916. More than 300 perished in the New London school explosion in 1937 and close to 600 in the Texas City explosion in 1947. Tornadoes in Goliad, Waco, and Wichita Falls claimed hundreds of lives, and the death toll from a 1985 Delta plane crash caused by wind shear was 134.

In addition to the disasters covered in individual chapters, Cox includes an appendix summarizing more than seventy-five other major disasters.

The stories, while sad, also relate how Texans have reacted heroically in the face of death and tragedy.

For a full treatment of the 1900 Galveston hurricane, read John Edward Weems' *A Weekend in September* (A&M, 1988).

# The Courthouses of Texas

## Mavis P. Kelsey Sr. and Donald H. Dyal

Texas A&M University Press, 1993, 2007

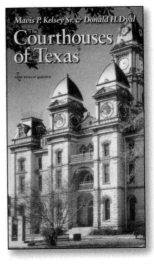

All 254 county courthouses in Texas are covered in this popular guide, each receiving one page with a color photo, construction date, county population, county seat, and a note about whom the county was named for.

In addition to the courthouses, presented alphabetically by county, the book includes an essay, "A Personal Tour of the Courthouses of Texas," by Dr. Mavis Kelsey, the Houston physician and courthouse connoisseur who conceived the idea for the book and even helped underwrite the first edition because he was afraid Texas A&M University Press would lose money on the venture. Instead, *The Courthouses of Texas* has become one of the press's all-time best-sellers. Also, at the back of the book, are three pieces about the naming of Texas counties and county seats. While no Texas county is named for a woman, several county seats are.

Another excellent book on Texas courthouses is *Historic Texas Courthouses*, a gorgeous coffee table volume featuring a hundred of the state's most picturesque courthouses. Published by Bright Sky Press in 2006, it is out of print, but if you can find a copy at a used book venue, snatch it up.

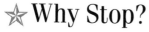# Why Stop?
*A Guide to Texas Roadside Historical Markers*

## Betty Dooley Awbrey and Stuart Awbrey

Taylor Trade Publishing, Sixth Edition, 2013

No one can drive very far on Texas roads or highways without passing a historical marker noting some event or person or place deserving enough to have a plaque dedicated to it. At last count Texas had more than 15,000 roadside historical markers, and if you tried stopping at many of them it would take you a long time to get to wherever you were going.

*Why Stop?* can help. It can't begin to catalogue all 15,000, but in the 500 pages of the sixth edition the authors cover more than 2,500 of the more prominent ones, giving the town, address, and the inscription on each marker.

*Why Stop?* was initially published in 1978 and has been updated about every six years since. When the book first came out, Texas had about 6,000 historical markers. With each subsequent edition, new markers were added, but others had to be deleted from the book to keep it a manageable size and price.

The authors say the purpose of the book "is to give readers the pleasure of learning about the colorful history of Texas without having to delay a trip."

Two companion volumes by Dan K. Utley and Cynthia J. Beeman—*History Ahead* and *History Along the Way* (A&M)—go into more depth concerning the stories behind selected markers.

# Some Other Notable Titles

⭐ In *West Texas: A Portrait of Its People and Their Raw and Wondrous Land* (Tech, 1999), Mike Cochran and John Lumpkin take readers on a rollicking tour filled with cowboys and coaches, cafes and con men, wildcatters and windmills, choking dust storms and stunning sunsets, rattlesnake roundups and prairie dog towns, generous saints and convicted sinners.

⭐ *The Amazing Faith of Texas: Common Ground on Higher Ground* by Roy Spence (distributed by UT, 2006) is a coffee-table book about a topic not often dealt with objectively in the Bible Belt—religion. In two-page spreads, Texans of various faiths give voice to their simple, yet often profound, personal beliefs.

⭐ *From Uncertain to Blue* by Keith Carter (1988; republished UT, 2011) resulted from Carter's year-long venture taking photographs in small Texas communities with colorful names, like Paradise, Fairy, Lovelady, Valentine, Notrees, Happy, Cut and Shoot, North Zulch, Looneyville, Sour Lake, Old Glory, Ding Dong, Dime Box, Frognot, and Noodle.

⭐ *Encyclopedia of Texas Seashells* is a 524-page encyclopedia by John W. Tunnell Jr., Jean Andrews, Noe C. Barrera, and Fabio Moretzshon (A&M, 2010) giving Texas seashells the comprehensive coverage they deserve. Each shell variety gets a fourth to a third of a page, with front and back color photos.

⭐ In his well-written *Galveston: A History of the Island* (TCU, 1998), Gary Cartwright calls his subject "the largest, bawdiest, and most important city between New Orleans and San Francisco." And he spends every page proving his point.

⭐ Fascinating history lessons can be learned from cemeteries, a point emphatically proven by Bill Harvey's *Texas Cemeteries: The Resting Places of Famous, Infamous and Just Plain Interesting Texans* (UT, 2003). The book covers the entire state, filled with photographs, rich anecdotes, and fascinating notes on the history made by many of the deceased.

⭐ *Lovin' That Lone Star Flag* by photographer E. Joe Deering (A&M, 2011) is a collection of photographs of the many creative ways that Texans display the Texas flag—on boots, spurs, caps, shirts, running shorts, arrows, golf balls, windmills, buckets, birdhouses, and steakhouses, among other uses.

☆ Greg Lasley, a retired Austin police officer, produced *Texas Wildlife Portraits* (A&M, 2008), a stunning coffee table book featuring close-up portraits of snakes, owls, cardinals, bats, spiders, hummingbirds, beetles, turkeys, alligators, ducks, prairie chickens, armadillos, coyotes, and jackrabbits, among others.

☆ *Of Birds and Texas* by Stuart Gentling and Scott Gentling with an essay by John Graves (UT, 2002) is a magnificent ten-by-thirteen book, with more than seventy-five full page color paintings of Texas birds and Texas landscapes.

☆ Texas has more species of hummingbirds (eighteen) than any other state. New Mexico and Arizona tie for second with seventeen. Altogether, nineteen different species populate the three states, and all are pictured, painted, and written about in an informative, full-color book, *Hummingbirds of Texas, with Their New Mexico and Arizona Ranges* (A&M, 2005) by Clifford Shackelford, Madge Lindsay, and Mark Klym.

☆ Of several full-color guidebooks to Texas wildflowers, *Wildflowers of Texas Field Guide* by Rick Bowers and Stan Tekiela (Adventure Publications, 2009) is perhaps easiest to use—organized by color—and the least expensive. Adventure has also published field guides to Texas birds, trees, mammals, and cacti.

☆ Marcia Kaylakie's award-winning *Texas Quilts and Quilters: A Lone Star Legacy* (Tech, 2007) showcases thirty-four heirloom quilts from all over the state and the history, culture, and craft they represent.

# LAW & ORDER

From the pioneering days when the Texas Rangers often made up the law as they went to headline-making murders and high-tech investigative techniques, Texas readers have had an ongoing fascination with crime. Bonnie and Clyde, UT sniper Charles Whitman, high society evil-doing, and slick swindles—the state has had its share.

It's no accident that ten Texas authors have landed on the short list for the Mystery Writers of America's Best Fact Crime Edgar Award over the years.

And don't overlook a celebrated list of novelists who write crime fiction set in the Lone Star State.

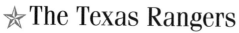

# The Texas Rangers
*Wearing the Cinco Peso, 1821–1900*

# Time of the Rangers
*Texas Rangers from 1900-Present*

**Mike Cox**

Forge Books, 2008–2009

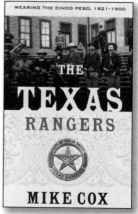

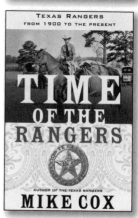

In two hefty volumes that trace the then-to-now history of the legendary Texas Rangers, author Mike Cox takes the reader on an anecdotal trip from the days when the rag-tag organization's primary purpose was to protect settlers from raiding Indians and chase down Mexican banditos to the high-tech, fine-tuned law enforcement agency it is today.

Moving well beyond the pulp adventure tales and B-Western portrayals, the first volume traces the birth of the nation's oldest crime-fighting organization, recalling days when those who served it were required to purchase their own horses and firearms. It was a renegade time on the frontier when the Rangers often made up their own laws and savage confrontation was the order of the day. Historian Cox doesn't shy from acknowledging that battles and lives were often lost. The period covered in *Wearing the Cinco Peso* was often dark and far from pretty.

In *Time of the Rangers*, Cox traces the story of the organization's growth and advancement into the modern age of cattle rustling, oil booms, Prohibition, and even World War II espionage. He moves the Rangers from horseback to helicopters, from borderland shootouts to scientific investigations.

And, while writing a well-researched narrative of this evolution, the author introduces a fascinating cast of characters who have served the elite agency.

Another notable two-volume history of the Rangers is Robert M. Utley's *Lone Star Justice* and *Lone Star Lawmen* (Oxford University Press, 2002, 2007; Berkeley Trade paperback).

# Go Down Together
*The True, Untold Story of Bonnie & Clyde*

## Jeff Guinn

Simon & Schuster, 2009

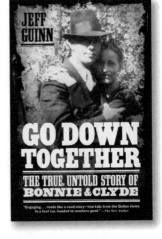

The twisted romance between Texas and its outlaws is as much a part of the state's history as oil booms, big hair, and political wheeling-and-dealing. And none has a more solidly etched place in its lore than the life and times of Clyde Barrow and Bonnie Parker. Even today, only their first names are necessary for immediate recognition.

In the hardscrabble Depression times, Bonnie and Clyde, dumb and dirt poor kids from the wrong side of the Dallas tracks, terrorized rural America with brazen acts of robbery and murder before a team of Texas Rangers finally ambushed them and put an end to the insanity.

In their short lives, the hapless criminals became darlings of a media that couldn't get enough of their illegal exploits. In death they became the subject of numerous books, applauded movies, and fodder for folklorists.

In his Edgar Award-nominated book, Guinn examines the era in which Bonnie and Clyde briefly captured the nation's imagination, offering up insights into the social struggles and changing times that gave birth to the rebellious bandit couple and their followers. The book is far more than a chronicle of two colorful criminals and their brief career. It is a story, well-written and exhaustively researched, that captures a bygone time in Texas history and lends it new understanding.

#  Gangster Tour of Texas

## T. Lindsay Baker

Texas A&M University Press, 2011

Texas historian T. Lindsay Baker offers a guided tour, complete with maps, photos, and directions, of sixteen of the most interesting and best preserved historic organized crime scenes in the state.

Baker begins with the most notorious gang of them all—Bonnie and Clyde and the Barrow Gang— tracking their various robberies, abductions, ambushes, and graves in a sixty-five page chapter. Other sections are shorter, usually in the range of fifteen to twenty pages, dealing with the Newton Boys, the Santa Claus Bank Robbery, Machine Gun Kelly, the Rum King of San Antonio, gambling in Galveston, and other organized crime activities.

To pull the book together, Baker said for several years he "prowled alleys, buildings, streets, sidewalks, and offices that had been the scenes of robberies, embezzlements, frame-ups, burglaries, moonshining, bribery, narcotics deals, and related murders and assaults. It has been a fascinating study, to say the least."

And a fascinating read. Thanks to Baker's sleuthing, you can relive those days from the safety of your arm chair, or at the very sites themselves.

Baker also is the author of *Ghost Towns of Texas* and *More Ghost Towns of Texas* (University of Oklahoma Press), providing readers with maps, photographs, and histories of fascinating bygone places, from abandoned Indian sites to towns that withered away not so long ago.

# A Sniper in the Tower

*The Charles Whitman Murders*

## Gary M. Lavergne

University of North Texas Press, 1997

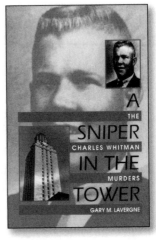

In that innocent August of 1966, the nation was not yet familiar with the concept of mass murders perpetrated by a lone gunman with only demented purpose. No school children had yet fallen victim to such horrors, no workplaces invaded by an armed and crazed attacker. Locales like Columbine, Fort Hood, and the U.S. Naval Yard were not yet an everyday part of the nation's vocabulary.

It all began when a crazed and well-armed young man named Charles Whitman positioned himself on the observation deck of the tower on the University of Texas campus and began a massacre that was to become an infamous part of Texas history. In only ninety-six minutes, the former Eagle Scout and ex-Marine shot forty-five strangers, killing fourteen, before he died at the hands of Austin police officers. The night before the ex-Marine had murdered his wife and mother.

Award-winning author Lavergne not only details the dramatic event but offers remarkable insight into the background that gave cause to Whitman's orchestrating the largest mass murder in American history at the time. Written with the benefit of hindsight and exhaustive research, it reaches far beyond the traditional true crime book. Lavergne provides a dramatic second-by-second re-creation of the horrific event as well as thoughtful analysis of the madness that might cause such a tragedy and law enforcement's newly energized efforts to deal with the monsters among us.

Lavergne also explores the case of another Texas murderer, Kenneth McDuff, in *Bad Boy from Rosebud* (North Texas, 1999).

# Blood and Money

## Tommy Thompson

Running Press, 2001

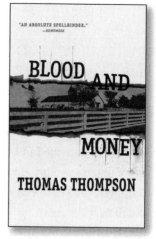

First published in 1976, the sensational story of a high society murder in the River Oaks section of Houston earned high praise from readers and reviewers and received the Mystery Writers of America's Edgar Award as the year's Best Fact Crime Book. And today it is still judged one of the premier non-fiction books ever written on a Texas subject.

If one ever needed proof that truth can be stranger than the most vividly imagined fiction, *Blood and Money* fits the bill. Its tangled cast of characters range from the beautiful daughter of a Texas oil millionaire and wife of an acclaimed plastic surgeon to gangland thugs, business wheeler-dealers, and an endless parade of medical experts and law enforcement personnel.

The victim, Joan Hill, and her obsessive and vengeful father, Ash Robinson, seem drawn from the pages of a Gothic novel in this well-written account that vaults light years beyond the true crime genre. And as their portraits are drawn, the reader also gets a close-up, and not always flattering, view of the city of Houston.

Toss in high courtroom drama, sex, hired killers, and the lingering questions such cases always raise and it is easy to see why Thompson's book has been labeled a classic.

While this is the definitive work on the famous case, it was Ann Kurth's book, *Prescription: Murder,* that was used as the basis for the television movie, *Murder in Texas,* which starred Texan Farrah Fawcett.

#  Lone Star Sleuths

*An Anthology of Texas Crime Fiction*

## Edited by Bill Cunningham, Steven L. Davis, and Rollo K. Newsom

University of Texas Press, 2007

Old West history aside, Texas novelists have found no more fertile ground to plow
than the field of crime fiction. And they've done
it so very well. Set in every part of the state with
excerpts written by men and women alike, *Lone
Star Sleuths* is an ideal sampler of the works of
many of the state's premier authors and a valuable
map to their expanded works.

The editors have included excerpts from thirty
outstanding crime novels, demonstrating a variety of writing styles, exploring
Texas geography from the big cities to the rural outposts and sharing every kind
of delicious murder and mayhem imaginable. If you're a fan of the genre, you'll
find old favorites here while learning of new writers you'll want to read. The list
is a Who's Who of Whodunnits: James Crumley, David Lindsey, Ben Rehder,
Rick Riordan, Rolando Hinojosa-Smith, Walter Mosley, A. W. Gray, Steven
Saylor, Bill Crider, Joe Lansdale, Neal Barrett, Jr., Doug Swanson, Jeff Abbott,
Kinky Friedman, Susan Wittig Albert, Carolyn Hart, Mary Willis Walker, D. R.
Meredith, Susan Rogers Cooper, and more.

What you'll find is that most have avoided the formula styles long associated with mysteries and given their novels a proper Texas twang and taste. An
excellent primer.

# ⭐ Texas Monthly on . . . Texas True Crime

## Editors of Texas Monthly

University of Texas Press, 2007

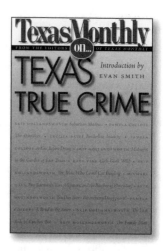

For all its award-winning reporting on social changes, eating habits, politics, finances, and high profile wheeler-dealers, *Texas Monthly* also does an exceptional job of keeping its readers abreast of the brutal and bizarre crimes committed within the state's boundaries. As Mike Cochran, author of *And Deliver Us from Evil,* once suggested, "We don't really have that much more crime here; it's just that we seem to do it better."

And in this twelve-story anthology, *Texas Monthly* writers like Skip Hollandsworth, Pamela Colloff, Cecilia Balli, Michael Hall, and Kathy Vine present a primer on crime reporting that takes the reader from the Panhandle to the Mexican border, deep East Texas to big city suburbs.

How can one not be drawn to pieces with titles like "Two Barmaids, Five Alligators and the Butcher of Elmendorf"? Or "Midnight in the Garden of East Texas"? You've got murderous drug wars, a jilted socialite that kills her husband by running over him three times, a body hidden away for months in a freezer, and the death wish of a West Texas teenager.

It is no surprise that Hollandsworth headlines the all-star cast of contributors with five of the dozen pieces. A gifted writer on virtually all subjects, it is when dealing with the state's darker moments that he shines most brightly.

After reading the collection—and its predecessor *Texas Crime Chronicles* (a Warner Books paperback no longer in print but easy to find)—you'll have earned a Master's in Lone Star State crime history.

# Some Other Notable Titles

✯ *Tracking the Texas Rangers* is a two-volume collection of thirty-one pieces by prominent Ranger historians, published by the University of North Texas Press (2012–13), which also has issued an excellent series of individual Ranger biographies. Readers interested in Ranger adventures, myths, and controversies will find plenty here to whet their appetites for even more.

✯ *Anatomy of a Kidnapping: A Doctor's Story* is Dr. Steven L. Berk's hair-raising memoir of his own kidnapping from his home in Amarillo one Sunday by a desperate man armed with a shotgun and needing money (Tech, 2011).

✯ *The Ashes of Waco* (Simon & Schuster, reprinted by Syracuse University Press) is author Dick Reavis' fascinating investigation into one of the most controversial and tragic events in modern Texas history—the 1993 raid of the Branch Davidian compound after a two-month standoff with religious zealot David Koresh.

✯ Disturbing though it might be, the folks wearing the badges don't always get it right. Investigative journalist Nate Blakeslee weaves a provocative non-fiction tale of a notorious undercover officer who destroyed lives and reputations in his *Tulia: Race, Cocaine, and Corruption in a Small Texas Town* (Public Affairs, 2006).

✯ Proof that modern-day Texas Rangers history is every bit as fascinating as recollections of the Wild West days is found in the stories of law enforcement legend Joaquin Jackson. In his *One Ranger: A Memoir*, and the sequel, *One Ranger Returns* (both from UT), he recounts memorable moments in his career in an honest and revealing style.

✯ Bill Neal, a former West Texas prosecutor and defense attorney, writes compellingly about Texas murder cases where the killer "managed to skate home free" in *Getting Away with Murder on the Texas Frontier* and *Sex, Murder and the Unwritten Law* (both from Tech).

✯ Bill O'Neal, not to be confused with Bill Neal, is the author of *The Johnson-Sims Feud: Romeo and Juliet, West Texas Style* (North Texas, 2010) revolving around the troubled marriage of fourteen-year-old Gladys Johnson and twenty-one-year-old Ed Sims in 1905. After a nasty divorce and contentious custody battle, Gladys gunned down Ed on the street in Snyder, triggering "the last blood feud in Texas."

★ *Famous Texas Feuds* by C. L. Douglas, first published in 1936 and reprinted in paperback by State House Press (2007), is a collection of stories about such bloody Reconstruction era feuds as the Regulators and the Moderators, the Taylor-Sutton Feud, the San Elizario Salt War, the Mason County War, and the Jaybirds and the Woodpeckers. See also C. L. Sonnichsen's *Ten Texas Feuds* (New Mexico, 2000).

# SPORTS

Bragging rights are the touchstone treasures of many Texans. You see it in the board rooms, political venues, and for certain, on the athletic fields. From the Friday night lights of schoolboy football to brim-full college stadiums on Saturday to Sunday's NFL wars, there are those who insist that football—*real* football—was a Texas invention.

Whatever the season, we celebrate our champions—in all sports. Such frenzied enthusiasm is clearly mirrored in the state's impressive literary archives.

# The Junction Boys

*How Ten Days in Hell with Bear Bryant
Forged a Championship Team*

### Jim Dent

St. Martin's Press, 1999

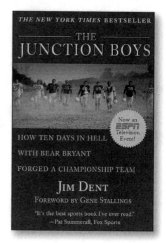

There is a very real danger attached to the business of writing a book whose subject is sports. The crutch of too many statistics, game scores, and press box clichés can result in something less than a literary masterpiece. Author Jim Dent sidesteps all such pitfalls in *The Junction Boys*, and as a result it ranks as one of the premier books on Texas football ever written.

Set in the summer of 1954, the book chronicles a hellish pre-season training camp conducted by newly hired Texas A&M coach Paul "Bear" Bryant. Two busloads of players arrive to participate in the sun-baked, torture-chamber practices near the Southwest Texas town of Junction. Only one bus was needed to return the survivors to College Station ten days later.

What Dent accomplishes is a highly satisfactory read, not just for the die-hard Texas A&M football fan or Bear Bryant admirer, but for anyone with an eye for a tale that takes the reader into the hearts and minds of a determined group of young men. To read the book is to know what the game of college football was all about in the mid-'50s and the lengths those who coached and played the game would go to be successful on Saturday afternoons.

Another highly recommended football title by Dent: *Twelve Mighty Orphans* (St. Martin's, 2007), the story of high school football in the '30s and '40s at Fort Worth's Masonic Home.

# Friday Night Lights
*A Town, a Team, and a Dream*

## H. G. Bissinger

Addison-Wesley, 1990

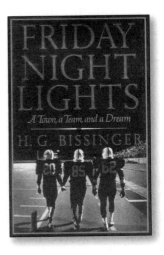

When H. G. "Buzz" Bissinger first visited Odessa in March of 1988, he quickly found many of the things common to mid-sized communities—economic woes, political infighting, problems with the educational system, trouble dealing with racial issues. As he would write, it could have been "anyplace in this vast land." Except for the one unique ingredient around which he would fashion a non-fiction classic: the residents of Odessa, Texas, were tightly bound by their enthusiasm for the Odessa Permian High School Panthers football team.

With remarkable insight, Pulitzer Prize winner Bissinger arrived from Philadelphia and saw things Texas reporters were too blinded by the lights to see. Odessa, no longer with an oil boom economy about which to brag, had become a town filled with second lien mortgages, overzealous fans, indifferent students, and lax teachers who too often judged their students' success by the scores on Friday night. And the visiting author wrote about it, producing a book that is as much social commentary as it is a sports story.

Upon its release, *Friday Night Lights* earned Bissinger few friends. What he had written was a warts and all reconstruction of a dramatic season in which the coach and players were subjected to unrelenting pressures. Still, the tradition-rich Panthers made it to the state finals.

The football season became the engine that drove a more ambitious undertaking. And whether those who call Odessa home liked it or not, the lifestyle of their West Texas town became familiar to millions of readers.

# Seasons in Hell

*With Billy Martin, Whitey Herzog and*
*the Worst Baseball Team in History*

## Mike Shropshire

Reprinted, University of Nebraska Press, 2005

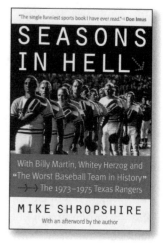

With Billy Martin, Whitey Herzog and
"The Worst Baseball Team in History"
—→ The 1973–1975 Texas Rangers

MIKE SHROPSHIRE
With an afterword by the author

First, they were the Washington Senators who nobody in the nation's capital really wanted. Then they moved to Arlington to become the Texas Rangers. And, while they would eventually grow into a couple of latter-day World Series appearances, they spent their early days on the south side of terrible.

In a candid and laugh-out-loud funny account of the 1973 to 1975 seasons, Shropshire recounts the few ups and many downs of a team of misfits that was as colorful as it was inept. When the book was first published in 1996, radio talk show host Don Imus called it "the single funniest sports book I have ever read." A lot of folks—Rangers management excluded—agreed.

Shropshire, a talented *Fort Worth Star-Telegram* sportswriter assigned to cover the team during those woeful days, describes major league baseball of another era—a time when players could booze with the best but couldn't bunt to save their lives; when fiery manager Billy Martin held court before turning the hopeless cause over to Whitey Herzog; when the players had names you don't remember.

For all its profane humor, ribald anecdotes, and daily misadventures, *Seasons in Hell* is an eye-opening look at the struggles of a franchise with visions of better days to come. Like Herzog said, "Defensively these guys are really substandard, but with our pitching, it really doesn't matter."

Few baseball books ever written are better.

# Hogan

## Curt Sampson

Rutledge Hill Press, 1996

In a state which has been, is, and forever will be blindly mad about its proud football accomplishments, Texas' greatest-ever sportsman may well have been a reclusive and talented golfer named Ben Hogan.

His professional career began in 1930 and lasted through four decades, and he won sixty-four PGA tournaments, including nine majors. And even as his achievements earned him a ticker tape parade in New York and the cover of *Time* magazine, few really knew the diminutive Dublin, Texas, native—until the publication of author Curt Sampson's bestselling biography.

Sampson succeeded in personalizing the man with a well-earned reputation as an icy and fiercely competitive athlete, going beyond the triumphs at the U.S. Open, Masters, British Open, and PGA to chronicle the hardships and heartbreak the man nicknamed Bantam Ben overcame during his lifelong pursuit of success.

He tells of the suicide of Hogan's father that prompted him to leave high school in his senior year to become a pro golfer at age seventeen, of his surviving a head-on auto collision at age thirty-six, and the remarkable comeback from the near fatal accident that won the hearts of fans worldwide.

From his days as an eleven-year-old caddy at Fort Worth's Glen Garden Country Club to his first professional tournament, the Texas Open in San Antonio, on to worldwide acclaim, *Hogan* takes the reader—whether a fan of golf or stories of man's unrelenting quest for greatness—on a remarkable journey.

# Wonder Girl
*The Magnificent Sporting Life of Babe Didrikson Zaharias*

## Don Van Natta Jr.

Little, Brown, 2011

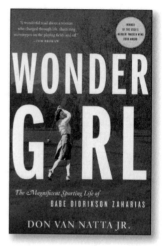

When *Sports Illustrated* named its top 100 athletes of the twentieth century, Babe Didrikson Zaharias was the only female in the top ten.

The incredibly talented, but sometimes controversial, golf and track legend who grew up in Beaumont, dropped out of high school her senior year in 1930 to play basketball for an insurance company-sponsored team in Dallas. She led them to the national women's amateur championship but didn't win many friends among her teammates, who were clearly unhappy with her hogging the limelight and boldly promoting herself.

Still representing the insurance firm, she single-handedly won the national women's track meet in 1932, winning six out of the meet's ten events. Then she went on to win two gold medals and a silver in the 1932 Olympics. A national superstar, Babe played various sports and even went on the vaudeville stage to earn money to support herself and her family. Then she decided to take up golf.

Again, she was a natural, but it took nearly eight years before she could break through the hierarchy that controlled women's golf and be allowed to compete, because she had taken money to play other sports. Meanwhile, she married a wealthy wrestler and promoter, George Zaharias, which gave her financial independence. When Babe finally hit the golf circuit, she dominated women's golf for the next decade until bouts with colon cancer sidelined her and finally took her life in 1956 at age 45.

# The Dallas Cowboys

*The Outrageous History of the Biggest, Loudest,*
*Most Hated, Best Loved Football Team in America*

## Joe Nick Patoski

Little, Brown and Company, 2012

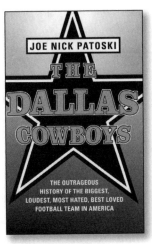

The difficulty with writing contemporary history is that it has changed even before the ink is dry. That said, in the half century the Dallas Cowboys have enjoyed a presence in the National Football League they have traveled through enough success and failure, triumph, tragedy, controversy, and praise to fill a bookshelf. Now, however, there is need for but one.

Author Joe Nick Patoski brings it all together in one volume, following the team from its inception in 1960 through the 2011 season. It's all here, from Dandy Don to Tony Romo, quiet owner Clint Murchison to bombastic Jerry Jones, stoic and successful coach Tom Landry to the parade of taskmasters who would follow.

The colorful, well-written history winds from the dismal early Cotton Bowl days to Super Bowl successes and into a home stadium so futuristic that it looks as if it landed in the midst of a sci-fi movie.

Patoski counts the money, details how the Cowboys became America's Team, and offers up fascinating profiles of the players and front office wheeler-dealers, blemishes and all. Authors of the book's subtitle would have done well to insert the word 'Complete," despite the fact the journey isn't yet over.

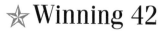# Winning 42
*Strategy & Lore of the National Game of Texas*

## Dennis Roberson

Texas Tech University Press, 1997, 2009

If you don't know what 42 is, then you must not have lived in Texas very long. It's a game played with dominoes by two teams of two players each. The teams bid against each other, and the team members work together to try to reach their bid or keep the other team from reaching its bid.

The name "42" reflects the fact that there are thirty-five points ("count") in even fives, plus seven hands of four dominoes per hand or "trick." The thirty-five points are the six-four, the five-five, the four-one, the three-two, and the five-oh.

Dennis Roberson's book on *Winning 42* was first issued in 1997 and has been updated three times, the latest being 2009. It includes basic rules, strategies, explanations, and variations on the game, which Roberson said was invented by two Texas teenagers in the late 1880s.

The game, he says, "is still played in rural feed stores and downtown county courthouses. It has been played by presidents, governors, singers, writers, and astronauts."

Two main strategies, says Roberson: 1. Offensively—Bid smart. Don't overbid your hand, learn to count on your partner, and take calculated risks. 2. Defensively—Never underestimate the skill of setting the bidder. Don't get in a bidding war against a team that overbids. Just set 'em!

#  A Thousand Deer
*Four Generations of Hunting and the Hill Country*

## Rick Bass

University of Texas Press, 2012

Rick Bass grew up in Texas and is highly regarded as a writer and an environmentalist, with nearly thirty books of fiction and non-fiction, most having to do with the habitat. A *Thousand Deer* is a collection of non-fiction pieces about deer hunting, most of them having appeared in magazines such as *Texas Monthly* and *Field & Stream*.

Despite the implications from the book's subtitle, the stories do not all take place in the Hill Country, or even in Texas for that matter. For years Bass, who still gets back to Texas often, has lived in Montana, and several of the pieces are set in Montana. Not that that should matter to hunters who share the writer's passion for hunting and for nature.

Most of the stories relate to family, past and present, like "Deer Camp" and "A Texas Childhood." "Mary Katherine's First Deer" is a poignant piece about a successful hunt with his oldest daughter. "Colter's Creek Buck" is about a hunt in Texas with his bird dog.

"I can't separate any discussion of hunting from a discussion of my family," Bass writes. "We've always hunted – my father, uncle, brothers, and I. We gather our food. We gather the years."

If you love hunting, there is much grace and beauty and depth in Bass's prose.

# Some Other Notable Titles

★ Joe Holley tells the story of one of the greatest quarterbacks of all time in *Slingin' Sam* (UT, 2012). Sammy Baugh was a TCU All-American credited with changing the game of pro football forever when he led the Washington Redskins to the championship his rookie year and went on to set records as a quarterback, defensive back, and punter.

★ *Hide, Horn, Fish, and Fowl: Texas Hunting and Fishing Lore* is an anthology of thirty-six stories collected by the Texas Folklore Society (North Texas, 2011). Stories like "The Big Fish That Didn't Get Away," "The Lore of Wild Hog Hunting in West Texas," and "Pranks in Hunting Camp" make this a good read for the avid hunter or fisherman.

★ It is no wonder that *Sports Illustrated* judged Pete Gent's novel *North Dallas Forty*, published in 1973, as one of the greatest sports books of all time. Following eight zany days in the life of a pro football player, the former Dallas Cowboys wide receiver provides a candid look at the game as it was played in the '60s. That his fictional team sounds a great deal like the early day Cowboys is no accident.

★ *Texas Baseball: A Lone Star Diamond History from Town Teams to the Big Leagues* by Clay Coppedge (History Press, 2013) is a 180-page overview of baseball in Texas, starting with the Houston Base Ball Club of 1861, early major leaguers from Texas, the Negro and minor leagues, and the state's two big league franchises—the Astros and the Rangers.

★ *Our White Boy* by Jerry Craft with Kathleen Sullivan (Tech, 2010) is a candid narrative about Craft's personal experience of playing two years for the Wichita Falls/Graham Stars black semipro team in the summers of 1959 and 1960. Craft says he was the first white player to play in the West Texas Colored League.

★ *Playing in Shadows: Texas and Negro League Baseball* by Rob Fink (Tech, 2010) is an indepth, straightforward history of the development of black baseball teams and leagues in Texas and the contributions of early-day black Texas players.

⭐ *Chasing the Rodeo* by W. K. Stratton (Harcourt, 2005) is not strictly a Texas book, although the author's home is in Texas—and rodeo is the official state sport. Stratton offers a compelling inside look at professional rodeo from a season spent on the rodeo circuit in the west, soaking up the culture while also searching for the "rodeo bum" father he never knew.

⭐ In 1992 Austin-based golf coach/teacher Harvey Penick and author Bud Shrake combined efforts on *Harvey Penick's Little Red Book* (Simon & Schuster, 1992, 2012), a small but enduring book filled with instruction and anecdotes provided by the man whose practical wisdom and insight into the game earned him the title "Socrates of Golf." It became the bestselling book on golf ever published.

⭐ Rob Sledge's *It's a Jungle Out There: Mascot Tales from Texas High Schools* (State House, 2005) is a Texas high school sports fan's delight. From the Winters High Blizzards to the Itasca Wampus Cats, Sledge explains how more than 1,500 schools came up with their team names. The book is packed with charming anecdotes and delightful trivia.

# FOOD AND DRINK

When it comes to cooking, or just eating, Texans have plenty of tasty choices.

We almost guarantee that the books in this section will make your mouth water for a bowl of chili, a platter of enchiladas, a rack of ribs, or a sizzling steak, washed down by a Shiner or a glass of Texas wine and topped off with a generous helping of bread pudding or peach cobbler.

Enjoy!

# ⭐ Texas Cowboy Cooking

## Tom Perini

Comanche Moon Publishing, 2000

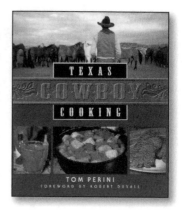

If you had to limit your collection of Texas cookbooks to just one book, this would be the one to keep. Published well over a decade ago, it remains as popular with Texas cooks—men and women—as ever.

Tom Perini is a working cowboy chef who owns and operates Perini Ranch Steakhouse in Buffalo Gap and caters celebrity events all over the country and even overseas. His steaks, his fried chicken, his hamburgers, and his beef tenderloin have won national awards and graced the covers of magazines.

His cookbook, even though it is billed as "cowboy cooking," encompasses a wide range of meats, side dishes, soups and stews, desserts, appetizers, and beverages—all beautifully displayed with color photos, lists of ingredients, easy-to-follow directions, and often accompanied by a story or two.

Take his fried chicken, for example, cooked complete with the pulley bone in a cast-iron skillet. He calls it "The Judge's Fried Chicken" because when a judge from Buffalo Gap sided with Abilene in moving the courthouse there back in 1878, the people of Buffalo Gap stole the judge's chickens and had a big dinner. So every week at Perini's, fried chicken is the centerpiece of the Sunday-only buffet.

Running a close second to the meat dishes are Perini's vegetable recipes—green chile hominy, cowboy potatoes, Zucchini Perini, ranch beans, and, of course, black-eyed peas. When it comes to desserts, Perini's bread pudding with whiskey sauce is legendary.

# Cooking Texas Style

*Traditional Recipes from the Lone Star State*

## Candy Wagner and Sandra Marquez

University of Texas Press, 1983, 1993, 2013

There's nothing fancy about this cookbook—no color pictures or anything—but it's been out there for thirty years and has found its way into thousands and thousands of Texas kitchens because it is a good, solid, down-home collection of Texas recipes.

The book represents a blending of the major cultures that have influenced Texas cooking, especially the Deep South, Mexican/Spanish, and German. So, in the poultry section, for example, you'll find a recipe for Texas fried chicken on one page, barbecued chicken Texas style on the next, followed by chicken chalupas, green enchiladas, cowboy chicken casserole, Mexican fried quail, and dove stuffed with sausage. The chapter on salads dressings, gravies, and sauces is a similar eclectic mix with ranch dressing, brown and cream gravy recipes, barbecue sauces, and picante and tomatillo sauces.

Other sections cover appetizers, drinks, soups and salads, meats, vegetables and side dishes, breads, and desserts. Seafood is in the same chapter with poultry and eggs, and there is a section devoted to pickles, preserves, and condiments, ranging from fig preserves and chow chow to pickled Pecos cantaloupe, German dill pickles, and jalapeño jelly.

With more than 300 recipes in all, an easy conversational style, and ethnic cuisine diversity, *Cooking Texas Style* will continue to be a Texas favorite for years to come.

# The Best from Helen Corbitt's Kitchens

## Edited by Patty Vineyard MacDonald

University of North Texas Press, 2000

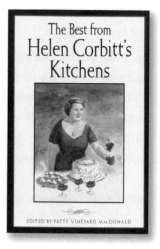

The Best from
Helen Corbitt's
Kitchens

EDITED BY PATTY VINEYARD MacDONALD

Patty Vineyard MacDonald selected dishes from Helen Corbitt's five cookbooks, plus some previously unpublished recipes, and produced a cookbook that would become the best-selling book ever published by the University of North Texas Press.

*The Best from Helen Corbitt's Kitchens* came out in 2000, more than twenty years after Corbitt's death. "My purpose in republishing this collection of Corbitt's best recipes," MacDonald wrote, "is not merely to preserve them, but to make them accessible and useful to a wider audience."

The book begins with a twenty-page biographical essay on Corbitt, who grudgingly moved from New York to Austin in 1931 but stayed to become a legendary Texas gourmet chef in Austin, Houston, and most prominently as the director of food services at Neiman Marcus and its legendary Zodiac Room in Dallas from 1955–1969. She died in 1978.

Corbitt's recipes, directions, and running commentary fill the next 350 pages, followed by five pages of snippets labeled "This and That." Sections are devoted to recipes for appetizers, beverages, soups and stews, breads, salads and dressings, poultry and stuffings, meats (beef, veal, pork, lamb), fish and seafoods, entrée sauces, cheese and eggs, vegetables and cooked fruits, potatoes, grains, pasta, and several chapters on desserts.

# ★ Jon Bonnell's Fine Texas Cuisine

## Jon Bonnell

Gibbs Smith, 2009

Upscale Fort Worth restaurateur/chef
Jon Bonnell has published two gorgeous cookbooks featuring enticing and exotic dishes like
Texas ostrich fan fillet with sherry-laced mush-
rooms, pheasant stuffed with goat cheese and
herbs in phyllo, quail ravioli, wild mushroom
and duck gumbo, and mountain elk tacos.

And that's just from his first book, *Jon
Bonnell's Fine Texas Cuisine*. In his second book,
*Jon Bonnell's Texas Favorites* (2012), are such rec-
ipes as chicken and cactus with southwestern romesco, deviled quail eggs, rabbit
corn dogs, and dove kebobs with mushroom gravy.

Of course, not all the dishes in the two cookbooks are that wild and crazy.
How about cast-iron cinnamon apple crisp, creamy grits with shrimp, grass-fed
Texas rib-eye with three-pepper compound butter, or grilled trout with mango
pico de gallo?

Whether you want to try cooking something new and exotic or just enjoy
drooling over the thought of eating such delicacies, Bonnell goes beyond your
typical chicken fried steak and barbecue fare to present Texas gourmet dining
at its finest.

# The Pastry Queen

## Rebecca Rather with Alison Oresman

Ten Speed Press, 2004

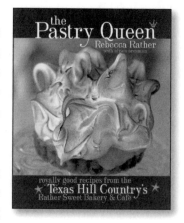

Known to her friends and customers as the Pastry Queen, Rebecca Rather published a wonderful cookbook with that title. At the time she owned and operated Rather Sweet Bakery & Café in Fredericksburg, which had begun in Austin a few years earlier.

"It's incredible that you can take flour, sugar, water, and eggs and make something that's unbelievably good," she writes. And she claims that her hands-on approach to baking is "easier than it seems."

The book is filled with such delectables as Fourth of July Fried Pies, Mrs. Chisholm's Divinity, Texas Pralines, Bananas Foster Shortcakes, Triple-Threat Chocolate Chip Cookies, Seventh Heaven Chocolate Truffle Cake, and the dessert featured on the cover of the book, Texas Big Hairs Lemon-Lime Meringue Tarts. Most of the recipes are accompanied by color photographs.

The cookbook is divided into eight sections, covering breakfast eats, muffins and scones; pies and tarts; everyday desserts and candies; desserts for special occasions and holidays; cookies, brownies, and bars; lunches and light dinners; treats kids love; and drinks.

Rather followed up this best-seller with two more books, *The Pastry Queen Christmas* and *Pastry Queen Parties*.

# A Bowl of Red

## Frank X. Tolbert

Doubleday, 1972; Texas A&M University Press, 2002

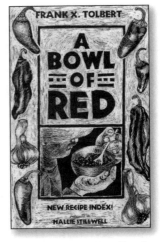

Be aware that it is not the filet or fajita, fish or fowl that is generally judged the most favored dish of Texans. That distinction, going back to days of Old West cattle drives and even when an Austin author named O. Henry featured it in one of his many short stories, is held by the steaming hot, sinus-clearing bowl of chili.

Ask any of the 10,000 or so members of the Chili Appreciation Society International or those who annually gather out in Terlingua for the World Chili Cook-Off Championship and they'll assure you that it is more than a food. It is a way of life. And their bible is Frank Tolbert's engaging *A Bowl of Red*.

A longtime columnist for the *Dallas Morning News,* Tolbert spent a lifetime gathering historical anecdotes, recipes, and profiles of chili heads hither and yon for the book that tells you everything you want to know about the spicy dish. And when it was re-released with an introduction by the late Hallie Stillwell, Big Bend rancher and author, offering up her own recipes and recollections, the book got even better.

In his light and folksy style, Tolbert not only takes the reader on a historical journey through the southwest and its growing love of chili but details the zany challenge that led to the first ever Terlingua Cook-Off forty-six years ago. It is left to Stillwell, one of the judges at that historic event, to set the proper tone for the book. She recalls that the Terlingua mayor, head judge of the competition, finally admitted that his taste buds had become paralyzed and thus declared the contest a tie.

# ⭐ The Prophets of Smoked Meat
*A Journey through Texas Barbecue*

### Daniel Vaughn

HarperCollins, 2013

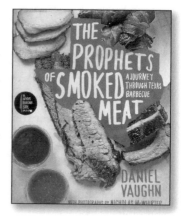

Whether you like to cook barbecue or just eat it, self-designated "BBQ snob" Daniel Vaughn's guided tour of Texas barbecue should whet the appetite.

Vaughn, a longtime barbecue blogger and the first-ever barbecue editor of *Texas Monthly* magazine, teamed up with photographer Nicholas McWhirter and traveled more than 10,000 miles sampling barbecue at about 200 Texas pits in a grueling thirty-five days, then published their findings in *The Prophets of Smoked Meat* with about 300 color photos to further tease the taste buds.

Eating and critiquing barbecue at as many as ten locations a day, Vaughn chronicled his journey region by region, inviting readers to come along and join them vicariously: "You won't have to drive 10,000 miles, defy the surgeon general, or abandon your family, but you will discover the heart and soul of Texas barbecue."

He included recipes or instructions from twenty-four Texas pit masters, but he warned readers that "the secret to the transcendent barbecue isn't in the ingredients but in the technique, a process they've repeated a few thousand times." At the end of the book, Vaughn didn't flinch in ranking what he considered the five best barbecue joints in Texas.

# Shine On
*100 Years of Shiner Beer*

### Mike Renfro

Bright Sky Press, 2008

If you can tell a book by its cover, then that's a good place to start in talking about *Shine On*. The cover (in the hardback edition) unfolds to become a twenty by thirty inch vintage Shiner poster. The book is billed as "the one coffee table book that looks better if you set your beer on it."

Shiner Beer is brewed at Spoetzl Brewery in the small South Texas town of Shiner, population around 2,000. The brewery was founded by German and Czech immigrants in 1909 and five years later was leased to Kosmos Spoetzl, an immigrant born in Bavaria. Spoetzl reigned from 1914–1950, and there have been just five brewmasters at the plant since.

The 192-page volume is filled with old and new photos of the brewery as well as color pictures of the various Shiner Beer bottles, cans, labels, and signs through the years.

A particularly interesting chapter in the history of Shiner Beer deals with the Prohibition era from 1918–1933. Most small breweries went out of business, but Spoetzl changed the production to a "near beer" and to ice. Renfro reports that old-timers around Shiner "will tell you without hesitation they never stopped making beer down at the brewery. They remember a ride in Dad's truck through town, with a stop at the loading dock to 'get some ice.' There was always that extra box or two that got loaded into the truck along with the ice."

# ☆ The Wineslinger Chronicles
## *Texas on the Vine*

---

### Russell D. Kane

Texas Tech University Press, 2012

Readers can sit back and sip a glass or two of Texas wine while enjoying Russell Kane's informal, informative, and entertaining tour of the Texas wine industry in *The Wineslinger Chronicles: Texas on the Vine.*

Kane, whose popular blog VintageTexas.com covers wine developments and events across the state, offers stories about Texas wineries and interviews with Texas winegrowers in an easy, conversational, down-home style.

At one stop on the tour—the Sweetwater Rattlesnake Roundup—Kane even does a wine pairing of Texas wines with rattlesnake meat. In the same chapter, before heading over to sip wine at a Comanche vineyard, he relates the horrendous historic story of an Indian raid and massacre near the town.

There are various guidebooks that offer tour information, times, maps, etc. on Texas wine, but Kane provides readers a come-along-with-me travelogue of the state's burgeoning wine country.

# Some Other Notable Titles

★ *Dining at the Governor's Mansion* by Carl R. McQueary (A&M, 2003) is a collection of 225 favorite recipes from Texas first ladies through the years and includes a healthy mixture of history about Texas governors and first ladies and the house they lived in.

★ *Fritos Pie: Stories, Recipes and More* by Kaleta Doolin (A&M, 2011) tells the story of Fritos Corn Chips, founded by the author's father, accompanied by more than 150 recipes.

★ Homesick for Texas food while living in New York City, seventh-generation Texan Lisa Fain started a popular blog that grew into *The Homesick Texan Cookbook* (Hyperion, 2011), a full-color 350-page tribute to the "bounty and joy that is Texas cuisine."

★ Trail driver Charles Goodnight is credited with inventing chuck wagon cooking, but Bill Cauble and Cliff Teinert have raised it to a whole new level of art with their full-color mouth-watering *Barbecue Biscuits & Beans: Chuck Wagon Cooking* (Bright Sky, 2002), covering a much wider range of dishes than Goodnight ever envisioned.

★ *Texas Eats: The New Lone Star Heritage Cookbook* by veteran food writer Robb Walsh (Ten Speed, 2012) includes more than 200 recipes representing a wide range of ethnic and regional traditions, as well as entertaining stories, profiles, interviews, and anecdotes—a book that is both an enjoyable read and a tribute to Texas cooking.

★ *Mex Tex: Traditional Tex-Mex Taste* by the late restaurateur Matt Martinez Jr. (Bright Sky, 2006) offers a variety of inviting Tex-Mex recipes praised for their taste, authenticity, and ease of preparation. Another good one is *The Tex-Mex Cookbook: A History in Recipes and Photos* by Robb Walsh (Ten Speed, 2004).

★ Terry Thompson-Anderson selected more than 500 recipes from about sixty-five Texas cookbooks by chefs and community organizations to put together *Lone Star Eats: A Gathering of Recipes from Great Texas Cookbooks* (Shearer, 2011), representing a wide range of culinary and cultural diversity.

★ *Texas Ethnic Cuisine: Stirring the Pot* by Dianna Hunt, one of the value-priced pocket-sized cookbooks from the Great Texas Line, includes more than eighty recipes from Native Texans, African American Texans, Norwegian Texans, Czech Texans, Mexican Texans, German Texans, Polish Texans, and Cajun Texans. Other miniature cookbooks from Great Texas Line include *Texas Church Supper and Family Reunion Cookbook*, *Tex-Mex 101*, and *Texas Morning Glory* breakfast recipes.

★ *The Big Texas Steak House Cookbook* by Helen Thompson and Janice Shay (Pelican, 2011) is just what it says it is—a book about some of Texas' most popular places for great steaks, sides, and desserts, with recipes and color photos.

# YOUNG READERS

Start 'em off early, we say.

Teach the kiddos their Texas ABCs. Fill their heads with a little Texas Mother Goose. When they're ready, introduce them to Hank and Old Yeller and work some Texas history into the mix. Then let them explore the wonderful, wacky weirdness of the state.

And, surely, they will grow up appropriately brainwashed—*informed*—and ready to take their place as fine adult Texas citizens!

# ☆ L is for Lone Star
## *A Texas Alphabet*

**Text by Carol Crane**
**Illustrated by Alan Stacy**

Sleeping Bear Press, 2001

With plenty of Texas children's picture books to choose from, parents should have no problem finding good bedtime reading for their young Texans.

*L is for Lone Star* goes beyond what a lot of picture books have to offer. Besides the ABCs of Texas—A is for Austin, B is for Bluebonnet, C is for Cowboys and Cattle, D is for Dr Pepper—the book also provides factual text sidebars on each page related to Texas history and culture. If the lilting lullaby of the rhyming ABCs doesn't soothe the kiddos to sleep, they can get an early indoctrination into Texas lore. You can't start too soon!

A few other recommendations for pre-schoolers and early elementary: *State Shapes: Texas* by Erik Brown, an informative book cut out in the shape of Texas. *Celebrating Texas* by Marion Dane Bauer is an inexpensive paperback with Mr. Geo giving a tour of the state. In the *Texas Activity Book* by Paula Ellis, children learn about Texas history and culture while working puzzles and coloring pictures.

# ★Texas Mother Goose

**David Davis**
**Illustrated by Sue Marshall Ward**

Pelican, 2006

Fort Worth author David Davis rewrote familiar Mother Goose rhymes to give them a Texas twist. The resulting verses may well be more entertaining to children's parents, who appreciate the parodies, than to the children themselves. But, hey, if the parents enjoy reading the books, their kids will probably get the message that reading is fun!

There is "Mary, Mary, from Old Granbury, How does your garden grow? With black-eyed peas and honeybees, it's quite a row to hoe." When Humpty Dumpty sat on a wall and had his great fall, Texas-style, "All the ranch cowboys and all the vaqueros got a big breakfast of huevos rancheros." When Jack and Jill go up the hill to drill for water, they strike oil instead. And there's the rewritten tongue-twister "Padre Pedro Picked a Passel of Peppers on the Pedernales."

The kids no doubt won't get the one about the "Three Blind Mice": "Three blind mice, See how they run! They ran for Senate up Austin way, since they're blind it's the place to stay; they're just like senators in every way, those three blind mice."

Another parody from Davis's pen is *Texas Aesop's Fables,* offering moral lessons with a decidedly Texas flavor, like "The Tortoise and the Jackrabbit," which teaches that slow and steady wins the race.

# The Original Adventures of Hank the Cowdog

## John R. Erickson

Maverick Books, 1983

John Erickson didn't set out to write children's books when he first penned stories about Hank the Cowdog, Head of Ranch Security, for ranch magazines. "My original audience consisted of adults, most of them involved in agriculture," he says. "I knew nothing about children's literature, and still don't."

Maybe not, but his *Hank the Cowdog* turned out to be a big hit with ranch families so he began self-publishing books in 1983. The series was picked up by a Texas publisher, then went national. It especially appealed to boys age ten and over, which made Hank extremely popular with elementary and middle school teachers and librarians. The children's book Erickson didn't set out to write became a hugely successful series for boys, with more than sixty books published and eight million copies sold. All titles remain in print and have also been recorded as audio books.

Bumbling Hank narrates the stories, filled with humor, a mystery, and a life lesson or two to be learned. Erickson himself owns and operates a working ranch outside of Perryton.

If *Hank the Cowdog* books appeal more to boys, girls might find a character they can relate to in the *Kylie Jean* series (Picture Window Books) by school librarian Marci Peschke. The chapter books are aimed at girls six to nine and feature Kylie Jean Carter, who loves pink, has a bulldog named Ugly Brother, lives in Jacksonville, Texas, and dreams of being a beauty queen. She's even perfected the wave.

# Old Yeller

### Fred Gipson

Harper Perennial Modern Classics, 2009

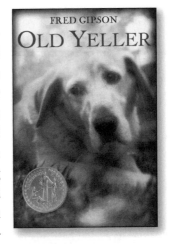

When, in 1955, author Fred Gipson submitted the manuscript for a juvenile novel he planned to call *Big Yeller Dog*, his editor wanted to change only two things. The book would be published for an adult market and its title shortened to *Old Yeller*.

One of the most beloved Texas novels, it did find a welcome audience among adults, but even greater enthusiasm was demonstrated by young readers. For that reason the Newberry Award winner is now touted as a classic read for children as young as ten. But regardless of age, the warmhearted story of a boy and his dog continues to delight readers from one generation to another.

It is a story so simply told as to be magical. Fourteen-year-old Travis Coates is left with the responsibility of helping care for his Hill Country family in the 1860s while his father is away on a cattle drive. Along comes a mongrel dog which Travis at first has no use for. But, as the pages flow, a kinship develops and Old Yeller finds a home, a friend, and a heroic purpose. It isn't a stretch to call it a love story. And while it would be a disservice to reveal the ending, suffice it to say it will require having a family-size box of tissues nearby. Walt Disney made the book into a highly successful motion picture.

Gipson's impressive body of work includes *Hound-Dog Man*, judged by many critics as his best novel. A coming-of-age tale, it traces twelve-year-old Cotton Kinney's awakening to the good and bad the adult world has to offer. To learn more about the author, read Mike Cox's biography, *Fred Gipson: Texas Storyteller*.

# ⭐ The Story of Texas

## John Edward Weems
## Illustrated by Tom Jones

Shearer Publishing, 1986

*The Story of Texas* is a 220-page history written for upper elementary and middle school readers and was published in 1986 in conjunction with the state's bicentennial celebration. It is written in an easy-to-read yet not condescending style and includes more than 125 black and white and lavish color illustrations, some of them full page or two-page spreads.

Except for the fact that it needs updating, it serves as a good basic history of Texas for children, written by a respected Texas historian whose other works include *A Weekend in September*, a Texas A&M University Press best-seller about the 1900 Galveston hurricane. Weems died in 1995.

Another Texas historian, Archie McDonald, wrote *Texas: A Compact History*, a 254-page narrative about the state's history. It is appropriate for middle school readers as well as adults and is more up to date since it was published by State House Press in 2007, but is not as richly illustrated as *The Story of Texas*. Historical topics and themes are dealt with in short, approachable segments.

# Journey to the Alamo

## Melodie A. Cuate

Texas Tech University Press, 2006

*Journey to the Alamo* was the first book in a series that uses the medium of time travel to teach Texas history to middle school readers. The novels revolve around a history teacher and his mysterious trunk that takes the youngsters back to the Alamo, where the famous battle is about to begin.

Subsequent books involve journeys back into time at Gonzales, Goliad, San Jacinto, LaSalle's settlement on the Texas coast, an 1840 Comanche raid at Victoria, and the Juneteenth celebration of the end of slavery. Fourth-grade teacher Melodie A. Cuate draws from travel and classroom experiences for each new episode in the innovative, award-winning series.

Another creative, award-winning approach to Texas history is *Voices of the Alamo* (Pelican, 2004) by Sherry Garland, beautifully illustrated by Ronald Himler. Garland sets the Alamo siege in historical context through the voices of characters before, during, and after the battle. Garland and Himler also teamed up on *The Buffalo Soldier* (Pelican, 2006), a picture book about black cavalry soldiers in the west after the Civil War.

#  Weird Texas

*Your Travel Guide to Texas's Local Legends and Best Kept Secrets*

## Wesley Treat, Heather Shade, Rob Riggs

Sterling, 2005

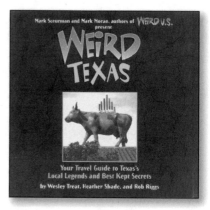

Texas is wonderfully weird, and *Weird Texas* celebrates that craziness in a full-color 288-page romp through the state's stranger claims to fame. You'll find the donkey lady, the headless rider, the alien plane crash, the cemetery statue of Jesus in cowboy boots, a collection of more than 700 toilet seats and lids, and the 142-foot-long outdoor sculpture of the musical score to "This Land Is Your Land."

And that's just a sampling. Section headers give a good flavor of what to expect, such as: local legends, ancient mysteries, unexplained phenomena, bizarre beasts, local heroes and villains, roadside oddities, haunted places and ghostly tales, and cemetery safari. It's the Texas bible of the bizarre—just let the book fall open to any page and start reading.

The book does not include maps or directions since many of the sites are on private property and others exist only in legends or, perhaps, imaginations.

In a similar vein, *Texas Redneck Road Trips* (Great Texas Line, 2012), *Texas Curiosities* (Globe Pequot, 2011), and *Oddball Texas* (Chicago Review, 2006) also mine the seemingly bottomless wonders of Texas weirdness. They do offer more details, like phone numbers, addresses, even web sites.

These books aren't just for young readers, but they do have a special appeal to middle school and up.

# Some Other Notable Titles

☆   *Batty About Texas* by J. Jaye Smith (Pelican, 2009, illustrated by Kathy Coates) is an informative and entertaining look at the Mexican free-tailed bat, the type that lives under the Congress Avenue Bridge in Austin.

☆   *Armadillo Rodeo* by Jan Brett (Putnam, 1999, Puffin, 2004) tells the story of Bo the baby armadillo who has an exciting day at the rodeo while his mother and brothers are searching all over for him. Ages 4–8.

☆   Joyce Roach teaches about the disappearing horned toad or horned lizard or just plain ol' horny toad while telling children a story about Tuck, Beam, Shine, and the rest of the gang in *Horned Toad Canyon* (Bright Sky, 2003), gently illustrated by Charles Shaw's watercolors.

☆   Children of all ages everywhere, not just in Texas, should get a kick out of Texas poet laureate Alan Birkelbach's collection of humorous, nonsensical poems, *Smurglets Are Everywhere* (TCU, 2010). The book, wonderfully illustrated by Susan J. Halbower, is worth reading for the verse "The Exhausted Woodpecker" alone.

☆   Kathi Appelt tells the story of *Miss Lady Bird's Wildflowers* (HarperCollins, 2005), illustrated by Joy Fisher Hein. A picture-book biography of the former First Lady and the beautification efforts she inspired, it includes a chart to help children identify roadside wildflowers. This book, of course, is best read in the spring.

☆   *The Legend of the Bluebonnet* (Penguin Putnam, 1983, 1996) is Tomie dePaola's prize-winning retelling of the classic Indian tale of how the bluebonnet, the state flower of Texas, got its name. A companion volume is *The Legend of the Indian Paintbrush* (1988, 1996).

☆   In *Luke and the Van Zandt County War* (TCU, 2002), award-winning author Judy Alter chronicles a unique historical afterthought from the Reconstruction days. When residents of Van Zandt County post notice that they would not only withdraw from the state but the Union as well, General Phil Sheridan and his troops come to deal with the rebellion.

★ Storytellers Tim Tingle and Doc Moore have teamed up on two books of spooky stories for middle schoolers—*Spooky Texas Tales* and *More Spooky Texas Tales* (Tech, 2005, 2010). Stories revolve around chupacabra, fang-bearing cattle, and a bowl of bloody oatmeal. Several of the tales were told to them by students during school visits by the authors. They're also the authors of a book of *Texas Ghost Stories* for adults (Tech, 2004).

★ Louis Sachar's *Holes* (Dell Yearling) became an instant classis when published in 1998. It won the National Book Award for Young People's Literature and became a popular Disney movie. The novel is about youngsters assigned to a juvenile correctional facility in a place called Green Lake, Texas, there to do an evil warden's secret hunt for buried treasure.

★ *When Zachary Beaver Came to Town* (Henry Holt, 1999) is Kimberly Willis Holt's bittersweet coming-of-age novel set in mythical Antler, Texas. Thirteen-year-old Beaver labors with the stigma of being called "the fattest boy in the world" and myriad family problems. The novel won the National Book Award for Young People's Literature in 1999.

# Conclusion

We have reached the end of our *101 Essential Texas Books*, but it is really just the beginning.

We hope you have found a number of books here that you will want to add to your own personal reading list, if not your library. Maybe our selections will encourage you to visit your public library or favorite bookstore and pick up some titles you may not be familiar with and see for yourself whether they add to your knowledge of Texas history, culture, and literature.

What we have tried to do here is whet your appetite for Texas books by suggesting 101 books—actually about 350 titles are mentioned—that we believe have helped shape and reflect the literary landscape of this great state.

Even though we have attempted to include a broad range of authors, titles, and interests, it would be impossible to list everyone's favorite Texas book or author. And even if we could, that ranking might shift with the next publishing cycle, the next up and coming writer, the next scholarly or popular blockbuster.

The Texas literary scene continues to evolve, and already on the horizon are influential new books and impressive new series being contemplated and developed by regional and national authors and publishers, with still others yet to be envisioned.

So this is a starting point, not an ending point. If it triggers some discussion (even arguments) about the books we have included—and not included—in our list of *101 Essential Texas Books,* then we feel we our effort has been worthwhile. If we have caused readers to want to explore the Texas literary scene more deeply for themselves, then we will take that as the ultimate measure of success.

Thank you, and good reading.

*Glenn Dromgoole and Carlton Stowers*

# Texas Book & Author Award Winners

## Texas Writer Award
(formerly the Texas Book End Award)
Texas Book Festival

Americo Paredes, 1998
A. C. Greene, 1998
Horton Foote, 1999
John Graves, 2000
Dr. William Goetzmann, 2001
Stanley Marcus, 2001
Bud Shrake, 2002
Bill Wittliff, 2002
Shelby Hearon, 2003
Elmer Kelton, 2003
Mary Margaret Farabee, 2004
Larry L. King, 2004
Walt McDonald, 2004
Sandra Cisneros, 2005
T. R. Fehrenbach, 2005
Cormac McCarthy, 2005
Louis Sachar, 2006
Mike Levy, 2006
Bill Broyles, 2006
Greg Curtis, 2006
Evan Smith, 2006
Dagoberto Gilb, 2007
Rolando Hinojosa-Smith, 2007
Robert Caro, 2008
Rick Riordan, 2009
H. W. Brands, 2010
Stephen Harrigan, 2011
Larry Wright, 2011
Tim O'Brien, 2012
Steven Weinberg, 2013

## A. C. Greene Award
West Texas Book Festival
Friends of the Abilene Public Library

John Graves, 2001
Walt McDonald, 2002
Elmer Kelton, 2003
Sandra Brown, 2004
Liz Carpenter, 2005
Jane Roberts Wood, 2006

Carlton Stowers, 2007
Don Graham, 2008
Kathi Appelt, 2009
Mike Cox, 2010
Wyman Meinzer, 2011
John Erickson, 2012
Jodi Thomas, 2013
Stephen Harrigan, 2014

## Lon Tinkle Award
Texas Institute of Letters

Tom Lea, 1981
John Graves, 1982
William Owens, 1983
Larry McMurtry, 1984
Donald Barthelme, 1985
Elmer Kelton, 1987
A. C. Greene, 1987
C. L. Sonnichsen, 1988
John Edward Weems, 1989
Marshall Terry, 1990
Margaret Cousins, 1991
Vassar Miller, 1992
Horton Foote, 1993
Americo Paredes, 1994
William Humphrey, 1995
Cormac McCarthy, 1996
Rolando Hinojosa-Smith, 1997
Robert Flynn, 1998
Walt McDonald, 1999
Leon Hale, 2000
William H. Goetzmann, 2001
Shelby Hearon, 2002
Bud Shrake, 2003
T. R. Fehrenbach, 2004
James Hoggard, 2005
William Wittliff, 2006
David Weber, 2007
Carolyn Osborn, 2008
Larry L. King, 2009
C. W. Smith, 2011
Gary Cartwright, 2012
Stephen Harrigan, 2013

## Texas Literary Hall of Fame

Friends of the Fort Worth Public Library

**2004 Members**
J. Frank Dobie
Horton Foote
John Graves
Shelby Hearon
Elmer Kelton
Larry McMurtry
Katherine Anne Porter
Walter Prescott Webb
**2006 Members**
Roy Bedichek
J. Mason Brewer
Sandra Cisneros
William Goetzmann
Rolando Hinojosa-Smith
William Humphrey
Dan Jenkins
Vassar Miller
Naomi Nye
**2008 Members**
Sandra Brown
Benjamin Capps
Betsy Colquitt
A. C. Greene
Tom Lea
William Owens
Suzan-Lori Parks
Edwin (Bud) Shrake
Bill Wittliff
**2010 Members**
Judy Alter
Bill Crider
Jeff Guinn
James Ward Lee
Bob Ray Sanders
Carlton Stowers
**2012 Members**
Sarah Bird
Carole Nelson Douglas
Robert Flynn
Leon Hale
Stephen Harrigan
Joe Lansdale
Rosalyn Story
Jane Roberts Wood

## TCU Book Award

Friends of the TCU Library

2001: Stephen Harrigan, *The Gates of the Alamo*
2003: Jeff Guinn, *Our Land Before We Die: The Proud Story of the Seminole Negro*
2005: Scott Zesch: *The Captured: A True Story of Abduction by Indians on the Texas Frontier*
2007: Timothy Egan: *The Worst Hard Time: The Untold Story of Those Who Survived the Great American Dust Bowl*
2009: Joe Nick Patoski, *Willie Nelson: An Epic Life*
2011: S. C. Gwynn, *Empire of the Summer Moon*
2013: Rick Bass, *A Thousand Deer*

# Index of Books and Authors

# About the Authors

## Glenn Dromgoole

Glenn Dromgoole is the author of twenty-seven books, including *A Small Town in Texas, Abilene Stories, West Texas Christmas Stories,* and *Good Night Little Texan.* A former newspaper editor in Fort Worth, Bryan-College Station, and Abilene, he has written a weekly column on Texas books and authors since 2002 and is founder and chairman of the West Texas Book Festival in Abilene. He was inducted into the Texas A&M Journalism Hall of Honor in 2000 and was named Abilene's Outstanding Citizen of the Year in 2013. He and his wife Carol own and operate Texas Star Trading Company, a Texas book, gift, and gourmet shop in Abilene.

## Carlton Stowers

Author/journalist Carlton Stowers has written more than thirty books on subjects ranging from sports to true crime. Twice he received the Mystery Writers of America's Edgar Award (for *Careless Whispers* and *To The Last Breath*) and he was presented the A. C. Greene Award for Lifetime Achievement in 2007. A member of the Texas Literary Hall of Fame and the Texas Institute of Letters, he has also been honored as a Living Legend of North Texas Journalism. *Dallas Morning News* book columnist Judy Alter listed his *Where Dreams Die Hard* as one of the Ten Best Texas Books. He and his wife Pat live in Cedar Hill, Texas.